GODDESS SYMBOLS

GODDESS SYMBOLS

Universal Signs of the Divine Female

CLARE GIBSON

BARNES
&NOBLE
BOOKS
NEW YORK

page 2, clockwise from lower left: representations of the Goddess archetype from contemporary Mesoamerica, ancient Egypt, Renaissance Italy and the Hindu pantheon.

left: Mycenaean figurine of a birdlike goddess (c. 1300 BC).

Contents

Introduction: Symbols of the Goddess

"I am nature, the universal mother, mistress of all the elements, primordial child of time, sovereign of all things spiritual, queen of the dead.... Though I am worshipped in many aspects, known by countless names, propitiated with all manner of different rites, yet the whole round earth venerates me."

From Lucius Apuleius, *The Golden Ass* (c. AD 160)
translated by Robert Graves

IN THE BEGINNING WAS THE GODDESS

Given the lack of historical evidence, it is difficult to know exactly when the human psyche first began to transcend the limitations imposed by a mundane, though essential, life of everyday survival to question its very existence and thus develop more abstract concepts of the sacred. Archaeological evidence, in the form of the cave paintings discovered in the Lascaux and Altamira regions of France and Spain respectively, indicates that humankind began to think both symbolically and "religiously" (the two are inextricably interlinked) during the late Paleolithic Age (around 40,000 BC). In depicting the bison, mammoth and horse upon which they depended for sustenance, these early hunter-gatherers were imbuing such creatures with supernatural functions; the various geometrical shapes that frequently accompany these images, however, are a more sophisticated expression of sacred belief. It has been postulated that the spirals, quadrangles, dots and lines with which our ancient ancestors decorated the walls of their caves are cosmic symbols, and moreover, that they are those of the Goddess. Since we know beyond doubt that many early cultures regarded her as the "mother of the animals," and because all these symbols later became associated with her, it is a compelling and persuasive

Opposite: The curvaceous limestone figure of the Venus of Willendorf is thought to date from between 25,000 and 15,000 BC. Below: A detail from the cave paintings at Lascaux, in France (15,000–12,000 BC), depicting bison.

Below: *A Goddess representation believed to date from the thirteenth century BC. Its winglike arms and beaklike head link it to the Goddess of ancient Europe, who was often worshipped in the form of a bird.*

Right: *An ancient Egyptian goddess incised in sandstone c. 700 BC; the hieroglyphics that flank her comprise a symbolic language used to describe her power and glory.*

interpretation. Indeed, when combined with archaeological finds from subsequent eras, such as the voluptuous Neolithic "Venus figures" (thought to date from between 25,000 and 15,000 BC) found in Willendorf, Austria, and at many other European sites, it becomes almost certain that early humankind worshipped the Goddess as the sole supreme being.

For those of a Western mind-set, who have been educated in the patriarchal systems of belief that have prevailed for centuries, it may require a great leap of imagination to understand why a goddess, rather than a god, should have been accorded such an unequivocal position of primary importance in the mystical beliefs of our ancestors. Yet her supreme status is, in fact, perfectly logical: in an era in which virtually nothing was known about human biological processes, women's mysterious, lunar-regulated menstrual cycles, as well as their awesome, and apparently autonomous, ability to give birth to new life, were perceived as proof of their magical powers. Men, by comparison, seemed virtually impotent, for it was then not even remotely suspected that they played a part in the conception and reproduction of human life. Thus, as concepts of the sacred evolved, it was entirely natural that the terrestrial world was seen as having a parallel in the supernatural realm, and that the supreme being was the Goddess—the great mother who created the cosmos (often from parts of her own body), and then the hierarchy of subordinate deities, humankind, animals and

birds, as well as trees and plants. In her gift alone lay the continuing fertility of all of nature's components, a power that was emphasized in the exaggeratedly well-developed bodies of the "Venus figures." Analytical psychologist Erich Neumann has described them as "representations of the pregnant goddess of fertility, who was looked upon throughout the world as the goddess of pregnancy and child-bearing, and who, as a cult object not only of women, but also of men, represents the archetypal symbol of fertility and of sheltering, protecting and nourishing elementary character."

If the Goddess was regarded initially mainly as the *magna mater,* or great mother, in the centuries that followed, she was recognized inevitably as a complicated entity in whom many other characteristics and powers of control were embodied. As Mother Earth, or Mother Nature, she could be benevolent if properly placated, and would ensure the earth's fecundity; if angered, however, she could manifest herself in the form of the Terrible Mother, bringing down drought and famine upon the world and thereby wreaking death and destruction. Not only did

THE DECLINE OF THE GODDESS

When humankind began to abandon hunter-gathering in favor of crop cultivation and husbandry, the significance of the Goddess underwent a corresponding adjustment, and she came to be worshipped primarily as a goddess of vegetation and domestic animals rather than as a protector and provider of animals of the hunt. Yet it was precisely this shift toward an agrarian society that heralded the eventual downfall of the Goddess, for in observing the breeding of their livestock, humans realized that the bestowal of the miracle of birth was not the sole province of women, but that men were necessary to the process of procreation.

Thus previously matriarchal societies became subject to the dominance of patriarchies, and the supreme status of the Goddess gradually became subordinated to that of a male deity. From being worshipped as a divinity of unrivaled power, she was gradually relegated to the position of the lesser consort of her initially inferior, divine "husband," until such monotheistic religions as Judaism and Islam finally banished her from their credos altogether. Indeed, by examining the surviving historical evidence, it can be ascertained that although the veneration of the Goddess was virtually universal by around 3000 BC, between 1800 and 1500 BC Judaism had begun to demonize her. By AD 500, when the newly Christianized Roman emperors ordered the closure of goddess temples, her destruction as the subject of official veneration in Europe and the Middle East was complete. Yet such was the resonance of the memory of the great Goddess that, in

*Left: Tauert, the ancient Egyptian mother goddess who was represented as a hippopotamus. Celebrated as a protector of babies during childbirth, she also had a chthonic role as conductress of those who had recently died to the underworld. **Below:** Raphael's* Justice *(1511) conforms to the classically inspired Renaissance convention of personifying abstract concepts or "virtues" as women. As here, Justice is usually depicted brandishing a sword of truth; she may also be blindfolded so that her sight does not prejudice her judgement and sometimes holds a pair of scales.*

she have a dual nature that reconciled such polar opposites as life and death, but she was also perceived as having a triple aspect: she was both separately and collectively virgin, mother and crone; creator, nurturer and destroyer; the ruler of birth, life and death. Thus she became an entity of astounding complexity and paradoxes: as the Greco-Roman Artemis/Diana, for example, she was worshipped as the pure lunar virgin, yet her insatiable sexuality was also celebrated in the myths of Cybele and Attis in Anatolia, or of Ishtar and Tammuz in Babylon, which related the great mother's embrace of a young, mortal son/lover—and his ultimate, and unavoidable, destruction.

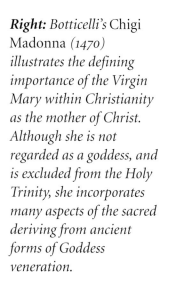

Christianity, for example, the Virgin Mary came to assume many of her characteristics (although Christians, and particularly Roman Catholics, among whom Mary's cult is strongest, would vehemently deny that she assumed the status of a quasi-goddess), while the veneration of Celtic goddesses—notably Brigit—continued, legitimized in Christian eyes by their canonization as saints.

However, in most non-Western established faiths—especially Hinduism—and in tribal cultures, the Goddess endured: she is worshipped today as fervently as ever and, indeed, in recent decades such "revived" systems of sacred belief as neopaganism and the Dianic tradition in the Western world have restored the Goddess to her pre-eminent position. Clearly, the Goddess alone fulfills an overwhelming spiritual need, but why? Why, despite the treatment to which she has been subjected, has this deity survived against the odds? And why is the Goddess such a powerful and universal symbolic entity across the collective spectrum of humanity's sacred beliefs?

Right: Botticelli's Chigi Madonna *(1470) illustrates the defining importance of the Virgin Mary within Christianity as the mother of Christ. Although she is not regarded as a goddess, and is excluded from the Holy Trinity, she incorporates many aspects of the sacred deriving from ancient forms of Goddess veneration.*

SYMBOLISM, THE ARCHETYPES AND THE COLLECTIVE UNCONSCIOUS

Carl Jung (1875–1961) believed that the answer lay in the human psyche. Although many other psychoanalysts and psychologists—notably Jung's erstwhile colleague, Sigmund Freud, the pioneer of the study of dream symbolism—recognized the symbol's power to evoke and influence our actions, both consciously and unconsciously, it was the work of Jung that would prove seminal in providing a compelling explanation as to why this should be so. While studying the various mythologies of the world, Jung was struck by the astonishing similarities of structure and imagery that many otherwise disparate sacred traditions displayed—even when there had been no crossfertilization of religious concepts and deities as occurred, for example, with the pantheons of Greece and Rome. Therapeutic sessions with clients, during which they spontaneously drew images of trees and mandalalike circles—both universal symbols equated respectively with the tree of life (or *axis mundi*) and wholeness—underlined this apparently innate human propensity for producing identical symbolic images, or mental blueprints. As a result of his observations and research, Jung propounded his theory of the collective unconscious and the universal archetypes that it contains, a theory that has since gained general acceptance.

Jung believed that the human psyche consists of three strata: the ego, or conscious mind; the personal unconscious, which relates solely to the individual's experience; and the collective unconscious, which is common to us all, and whose contents are universal and hereditary. The contents of the collective unconscious, Jung argued, manifest themselves in the forms of symbolic images, or archetypes, representing the primordial events that shaped human history. These archetypal images, which include such symbols as the mother and father, or the moon and the sun, are common to all people, whatever their personal or cultural experience and inheritance. It is precisely such archetypes—mother, father, hero, heroine, god and goddess, or shadowy trickster—that are given life and expression in the world's mythologies and cosmogonies (thus demonstrating what Jung termed humanity's "natural religious function") in an attempt to explain the reasons behind the creation and future direction of both the cosmos and humanity. Given the inherent ability of the human collective and personal unconscious to communicate with the conscious mind by means of the transmission of such archetypal images—either during the dream state, or by eliciting strong, sometimes irrational, emotions during periods of consciousness—it is logical that symbols of all kinds should evoke profound responses in us, for by tapping into the legacy of the collective human experience they speak to our instincts, as well as to our conscious and rational minds.

Symbolism is, then, a truly international form of communication, for it bypasses the barriers of language, race and culture, speaking directly to each level of the human psyche, but most meaningfully to the collective unconscious. When we view a symbol, say, an image of the moon, we recognize it on a conscious level, equating it to the astral body that shines at night; our personal unconscious may also recall a particular night with which, for whatever reason, we associate the moon strongly. Our collective unconscious, however, transcends such superficial connotations: in accordance with a more profound, metaphysical response, it associates the symbol with the tides, water and feminine fertility, but also with coldness, death and the underworld, and thus, since all of these are her attributes, with the Goddess.

Quite apart from its ability to awaken our deeply buried, instinctive responses, symbolism, considered on a rational level, is perhaps the most effective form in which sacred concepts can be given expression. How better could an abstract, intangible supernatural being, such as the Goddess, be represented than through the symbolic representation of her powers and characteristics? Verbal and written language are inadequate for the task, hampered as they are by strictures of grammar and ambiguity of interpretation, whereas a symbol—be it an iconic or aniconic pictorial image, a fragrance, a sound, a creature, or any other feature of the natural world—is instantly registered, recognized and reconciled. Furthermore, we have inherited the archetypes of the collective unconscious from ancestors who, in ancient

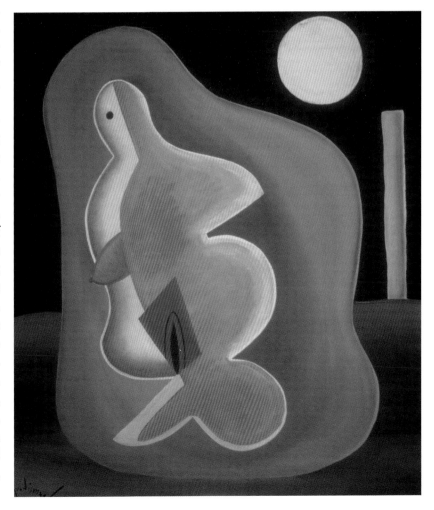

Below: In this untitled painting (1935) by Surrealist artist Ortiz, an amorphous but clearly female form, reminiscent of the ancient "Venus figures," appears in association with the moon. Through their work, the Surrealists enthusiastically promoted the theories of such pioneering psychoanalysts as Freud and Jung regarding the archetypes within the unconscious mind.

cated in life. And, as sacred concepts developed, symbols were often deployed to represent deities in hybrid, part-human and part-animal form, as seen in the mermaid, thus emphasizing their supernatural abilities as well as their dominant qualities. Symbols also served to proclaim a nebulous element of faith and hope (the crescent moon, for example, representing fertility); or to protect adherents of a clandestine religion from detection and persecution, and also to maintain the secrecy deemed necessary for its efficacy (ears of corn, for example, being the primary symbol of the Eleusian mysteries devoted to Demeter). Yet unless a fervent belief in the sacred concepts that underlie such symbols is maintained, the symbol loses its emotive power: pearls, for example, are now generally regarded in a prosaic materialistic light as jewels with a monetary value, rather than in their original sacred guise as bearers of the lunar and aqueous qualities of the Goddess.

Jung identified the most fundamental archetypes as the Anima, the symbol

Above: The Renaissance master Leonardo da Vinci's study Woman in Profile *has a strikingly serene and gentle aspect. It was probably undertaken in preparation for a portrait of the Madonna, who, in Christian tradition, exemplifies these qualities as a benevolent intercessor.*
Right: *The Maternal Kiss, by Mary Cassatt, reflects one of the Goddess's most important functions: that of giving and nurturing life.*

times, found it natural to think in terms of analogy, and who also believed that every aspect of the natural world was the effect of sacred, supernatural causes.

The emergence of symbolism and sacred beliefs was probably simultaneous, as early humankind sought to represent and influence the supernatural powers that they believed were responsible on the one hand for fecundity and well-being, and on the other for drought, death and suffering. It is understandable—even to the modern mind—that by representing an abundance of animals on the walls of the caves that sheltered them, early humans were expressing a wish (in religious terminology, a prayer) that such depictions should be repli-

JEANNE WALKER ROREX ©

Left: *The evocative* Contented Hands *(1989), by Cherokee artist Jeanne Walker Rorex, appears to express the gentle, yet powerful, influence of the Goddess, as symbolized by one of her primary universal attributes, the moon. She remains an important figure in tribal sacred belief, in sharp contrast to her degradation in the Western world.*

these archetypes with mythological figures, went further, stating that "the Great Goddess is the incarnation of the Feminine Self that unfolds in the history of mankind as well as in the history of every individual woman." Drawing upon the lessons of the past, he urged the conscious promotion of the Anima, arguing that the "one-sided patriarchal development of the male intellectual consciousness" had created the "peril of the present day." And "Western mankind must arrive at a synthesis that includes the feminine world—which is also one-sided in its isolation. Only then will the individual human being be able to develop the psychic wholeness that is urgently needed if Western man is to face the dangers that threaten his existence from within and without," he continued, in his work *The Great Mother: An Analysis of the Archetype* (1955). Indeed, the recent revival of the cult of the Goddess in the Western world, despite centuries of repression, appears to attest to a latent and deep-rooted need that she alone can fulfill.

Above: *The pronounced curves of this ideal medieval image from a Book of Hours celebrates childbearing.* **Right:** *In ancient times, the pearly mistletoe berry was associated with the moon, which it resembles in both shape and color.*

encompassing the rich variety of the feminine principle, and its masculine counterpart, the Animus. Both, he stated, are present within every human psyche, regardless of physical gender. He believed that the Anima and Animus (both of which psychologist Jean Shinoda Bolen regarded as present in the Goddess) had to be in balance before a person could achieve psychological individuation, or psychic "wholeness." Erich Neumann, in equating

THE SYMBOLS OF THE GODDESS

It is probably no accident that human-kind's earliest symbols were inscribed on the walls of caves, for the cave itself, upon which early hunter-gatherers were so dependent for shelter, is a symbol denoting the secure womb of Mother Earth. The cave may also be termed the cosmic "navel," in other words, the remnant of the umbilical cord that once connected all life to the universal generative womb. Other profound symbols connected with fertility and cosmic creation include the egg, the seed, the web-spinning spider and the primeval waters, all of which are among the primary representations of the Goddess. The tree of life is another such symbol, which, along with the mountain or hill—whose shape recalls the divine breast—may also be equated with the *axis mundi*, or cosmic axis, the pole that links the underworld, earth and the heavens. (Because of its phallic shape, some commentators regard the *axis mundi* as being a masculine symbol, but it is more properly associated with the Goddess, who is the demiurge of every component of the natural world. Furthermore, in ancient Greek, Roman, Celtic and Germano-Norse mythologies, the guardians of the water of life that flows below the tree of life—the Fates—were always female.) The fertile earth is clearly symbolic of the creative powers of the Goddess's body, and it is sig-

nificant that two Latin phrases denoting a mystical communion with the earth relate to both the Goddess and the fundamental feminine archetype: *anima mundi* ("spirit of the world") and *anima loci* ("spirit of the place").

Although in some cultures, including the Japanese Shinto tradition, whose most important deity is the solar goddess Amaterasu, she is associated with the sun, the moon is one of the most important

Left: Eggs are among the Goddess's leading symbols, for they enclose and protect the embryonic bird.
Below: Both the moon, which regulates the oceanic tides, and water are primary attributes of the Goddess, symbolizing her power over the cycle of life, death and rebirth.

universal symbols of the Goddess. In ancient times, the moon goddess was venerated for her mysterious ability to influence both women's menstrual cycles and the ebb and flow of the tides. The waxing and waning of the moon was equated with the inexorable passage of birth, life, death and then rebirth, over which the moon goddess was believed to have control. Even when the Goddess was dispossessed by a male deity personified in the fiery masculinity of the sun, she retained her lunar association. Thus certain creatures became sacred to her, including dogs (also symbolic of the hunt), who howl at the moon; cats, whose pupils were perceived to mimic the action of the moon's phases; and the toad and hare (who also have strong connotations of fecundity), which many disparate cultures believed to live in the moon.

Circular, silvery and iridescent pearls and opaque mistletoe berries are lunar symbols by association, their whiteness also being connected with the purity of the Goddess in her virgin aspect and with the Goddess of death (for the pale moon is a dual symbol, denoting both the darkness of night and the bleached color of bone). Stars, too, may represent the Goddess: Venus, for example, the deity of the Morning Star, who, along with the Virgin Mary, was termed *Stella Maris* (star of the sea).

Water in all its forms—whether as ocean, river, stream, well, or fountain—is another unequivocal symbol of the Goddess, for it is both influenced by the

moon and a source of life, harboring a multitude of aquatic creatures and sustaining terrestrial animals and plants. Fishes (whose oval shapes, like those of shells, almonds and the Hindu *yoni* symbol, recall the fundamental physical manifestation of femininity) are clear Goddess symbols, along with such egg-laying waterbirds as ducks, swans, geese and cranes. Probably the most important symbol associated with water is the snake, whose sinuous meandering reflects the movement of watercourses. The serpent's claim to Goddess symbolism is underlined by the fact that it sheds its skin periodically, in mystical terms emerging renewed and reborn. Vessels of all kinds, notably the cauldron of plenty that is such a significant feature of both Celtic mythology and the quasi-Christian tales of the Holy Grail, are also attributes of the Goddess, for they contain life-giving water and may also be equated with the shape and function of the womb.

In her maternal aspect, the creatures most closely associated with the Goddess are the fiercely protective bear, the fecund domestic pig, and the milk-producing cow. Grain (or the bread made from it), maize, and rice are primary universal attributes from the botanical world, expressing her ability to create and sustain life by providing humanity with staple foods. In ancient Egypt, the Indian Sub-

Above: Flora was the Roman goddess of flowers and the spring, a pleasure-loving deity who was celebrated during the riotous Floralia festival which heralded the re-awakening of nature after its long winter sleep. **Right:** *The peach—like the apple in the West, a symbol of immortality—is among the primary attributes of many Far Eastern goddesses, for not only is its flesh sweet and succulent, but its shape can be equated with female sexuality.*

continent and the Far East, the lotus is most frequently a symbol of the Goddess, for not only is it regarded as possessing perfect beauty, but it is rooted in the muddy waters. In Europe, the Goddess was said to grow the apples of immortality in her garden of paradise; in the Far East, peaches assume this symbolism. Another fundamental symbol of the Goddess's vitality is the blood that courses through all creatures' veins (and early humans must have marveled at the female menstrual cycle, during which blood, but not life, was lost). That blood was associated with the Goddess in ancient times is attested to by the fact that archaeologists working in Czechoslovakia and Iraq recovered bodies that had been ceremonially coated in red ochre before burial. These grave finds are estimated to date from between 12,000 and 9,000 BC, but even today, Hindu devotees of the Goddess smear their hands in red henna to acknowledge and affirm her life-giving powers. Yet blood is also a symbol of wounding and, indeed, of death itself, and burial in the fertile black earth of the tomb may be regarded as a return to the womb of the Goddess, from which she may grant rebirth to the fortunate.

These are but a few of the multitude of symbols sacred to the Goddess. The fact that all are drawn from the natural world testifies to her holistic nature, within which apparently unrelated components are united in a symbiotic and self-perpetuating cosmic relationship. Thus she gives life to all things, sustains it, and then, of necessity, destroys it so that new life may burgeon. Thereby, she teaches what modern society is only beginning to relearn (although tribal societies have never forgotten it): that no single aspect of nature is separate or superior, and that a harmonious natural balance must be maintained if Mother Earth, and all the life forms that she embodies and supports, is to survive.

ABOUT THIS BOOK

Since the dawn of time, many thousands of goddesses—all of whom represent individual aspects of the Goddess—have been the object of worship; furthermore, the names of thousands more have inevitably vanished into the mists of history. Indeed, there are so many Goddess incarnations that many of her lesser forms—such as nymphs, demons, maenads and natural spirits—have had to be omitted from this book. However, it presents a representative selection of some of the most important manifestations of the Goddess, roughly categorized by date and by the geographical and/or cultural areas of her devotees. Through the multitude of symbols outlined, which are given meaning within the context of their culture, readers will gain a comprehensive introduction to the complex characteristics and powers of the Goddess, and will, perhaps, be inspired to learn more about this most ancient, universal and remarkable supreme deity who, although still venerated in the rites and traditions of many other sacred cultures, has only now re-emerged into the consciousness of the Western world.

Below: In Greco-Roman sacred belief, the maenads were nymphs who attended Dionysus (Bacchus). This bas-relief is a Roman copy of a Greek prototype dating from the fifteenth century BC; the languid maenad clasps the staff (thyrsus) of the god entwined with ivy and crowned by a pine cone symbolizing fecundity.

Mesopotamian, West Semitic and Phrygian Civilizations

S uch is the importance of the sacred beliefs of the Near Eastern Mesopotamian civilizations, as well as those of Syria, Palestine and Anatolia, that they have been collectively called "the cradle of civilization." Their mythologies are among the earliest recorded, and scholars have revealed that, telling as they do of cosmic battles between entities of good and evil, and the "death" and "rebirth" of the deity of vegetation, they may be regarded as archetypal cosmogonies whose influence continues to reverberate down the millennia. The Goddess played a leading role within these mythologies, and although she occasionally revealed a gentle aspect, she was celebrated mainly as a demanding and jealous entity, a leonine patroness of war whose power was such that men were severely imperiled if they disregarded it (indeed, to qualify as the priestly servants of the Anatolian Cybele, men were required to castrate themselves). And despite the fact that the Goddess had been venerated in Europe since the dawn of time, it was the legacy of these ancient civilizations, spread northward through the catalyst of Greco-Roman mythology, that influenced significantly the sacred beliefs of the entire continent.

THE MESOPOTAMIAN GODDESS

The geographical area that made up the Near Eastern region of Mesopotamia was "the land between the rivers" Tigris and Euphrates. From this fertile breeding ground, a successive series of remarkably sophisticated societies emerged, each inheriting and preserving elements of the sacred belief of its predecessor, while introducing its own local deities into the general Mesopotamian pantheon. It was the independent city-states of Sumeria that, between around 3000 and 250 BC, first began to unite into a coherent political unit, and to standardize their multitude of sacred beliefs. And, although each city retained its personal deity, to whom homage was paid in the pyramidal ziggurats (which symbolized the cosmic mountain— the body of the Goddess) that dominated it, seven deities gradually attained positions of supremacy throughout the whole of Sumeria.

According to the Sumerian mythology, the cosmos was created from the primeval waters—that is, from the body of the Goddess Nammu. It was she who gave birth to the cosmic mountain, An-Ki,

Opposite: According to many Mesopotamian myths, the cosmos was created from the primeval waters, as personified by such goddesses as the Sumerian Nammu and the Babylonian Tiamat. The Canaanite Ahirat and Syrian Atargatis were also equated with the sea.

Left: An ancient image identified as a mother goddess by her prominently rounded torso and breasts. Mesopotamian deities like the Sumerian Ishtar and the West Semitic Astarte were often depicted in this form.

which in turn created Enlil, the air god, who forcibly separated his entwined parents, thus producing two divine entities: An—the masculine air god—and Ki—the feminine earth goddess. Other myths tell that the god who assumed Nammu's original power over the water was Enki; and that the goddess Ninhursag assumed Ki's role as the mother of the deities and the goddess whose realm was the earth. Three additional deities ruled over the heavens: Nanna, the moon god (the son of Enlil), Utu, the sun god (son of Enlil's consort Ningal), and Inanna, goddess of the Morning and Evening Star (the planet Venus). Rulership of the underworld, Irkalla, was once the sole responsibility of the goddess Erishkigal, but myths relate that when Erishkigal, who was unable to leave her gloomy province to partake of the deities' heavenly feast, sent her messenger, Namtar, to bring back her share, the terrible solar deity, Nergal, insulted him, thus causing Erishkigal to challenge him to combat. Nergal overcame the goddess, and the two finally united to rule the underworld together. Despite the fact that she was the goddess of death, Erishkigal was also regarded as having a benevolent aspect, for it was she who released the mineral wealth of the earth in order to enrich humans.

Although it may appear that the primary Sumerian goddesses—Ninhursag, Inanna and Erishkigal—were lesser deities who submitted to their male counterparts and accepted the leadership first of An and then of Enlil, they were, in fact, the object of intense devotional cults and wielded immense power. In common with her daughters, Ninhursag had a number of names, forms and functions. As Ninsikilla ("pure lady"), she was the virgin queen of paradise and immortality; following her union with Enki, she was known as Damgalnunna ("wife of the prince"); and as the mother of the gods, Nintuama Kalamma (or "lady who gives birth"). However, it was as Ninhursag, the earth mother and mother of (cosmic) mountains, that she was especially venerated, and in this incarnation she was symbolized by the cow, or by the cow's horns, which, by virtue of their shape (for they are reminiscent of Fallopian tubes) also represented her womb. She was regarded as a fierce protectress of vegetation, as is illustrated by the tale describing her fury when her husband, Enki, consumed some of her cherished plants: his punishment was death, but after a time, she relented and created eight deities to heal each of his vital organs, thus reviving the god of the waters (this myth may refer to a historical drought).

Ninhursag—the creator of vegetation—and the queen of the dead, Erishkigal, were each potent manifestations of the Goddess's powers, but perhaps the greatest Sumerian goddess was Inanna, who combined the main functions of her mother and elder sister, and was worshipped chiefly as the goddess of sexual love, fertility and war. Various myths tell of Inanna and her son/lover, Dumuzi ("faithful son"). In one version, after the mortal Dumuzi died, she traveled to the underworld realm of her sister, Erishkigal, to rescue him, but found her way barred by the gate of the "land of no return"; her threats to break it down and release the shadowy subjects of Erishkigal forced her sister to let her pass. At each of the seven successive gates that led to Erishkigal's inner sanctum, Inanna was divested of an article of adornment: her heavenly crown, earrings, necklace, brooches, belt, bracelets, and, lastly, the cross that "covered her femininity." Finally, the naked Inanna was received by her hostile sister, who not only derided her nudity, but ordered the demon Namtar to bind and torture her with the "sixty miseries of eyes, heart and head." As a result of her incarceration, all vegetation on earth withered and died, causing the gods to send their messenger, Asushanamir, to order her release. Erishkigal complied reluctantly, and, after having Namtar sprinkle Inanna with the water of life, she was led to freedom, thus restoring fertility to the world. Another version of the myth relates that after the jealous Erishkigal murdered her beautiful sister, their parents, Enki and Ninhursag, arranged for Dumuzi (who had not mourned the loss of Inanna) and his sister Gestinanna (who is equated with the vine) to take her place, each spending half

the year in the land of the dead. Both Inanna and Dumuzi are sometimes called "the green one," and these myths illustrate clearly the belief that without Inanna's presence, no life can thrive on earth, and to ensure the world's continuing fertility, her beloved son/lover must be sacrificed.

When King Hammurabi (1762–50 BC) conquered Sumeria, he united the various city-states into a new empire: Babylonia. Despite their victory, the Babylonians largely retained the Sumerian pantheon, albeit giving the old deities new names. Thus the Sumerian goddess Inanna became Ishtar, and her lover, Dumuzi, Tammuz. An important new addition to the Mesopotamian divine family was the supreme god Marduk, the Babylonian national deity, whose ascendancy is related in the Enuma Elish. According to this epic, the gods were

Left: The Mesopotamian goddess Inanna/Ishtar, riding a lion and armed with weapons, in keeping with her martial aspect. Her other attributes include the lunar crescent, the all-seeing eye and the serpent.

Right and below: The serpentine symbol of fecundity (right) was sacred to such Near Eastern deities as the Elamite mother goddess and Atargatis of Syria. Its fertility symbolism derives from its association with water, as seen, for example, in its link with the Babylonian Tiamat, goddess of salt water, who created legions of serpents to help her avenge the death of her consort. Tiamat's other representation, as a dragon (below), had a major influence on the myths of later cultures.

Background: The eight-pointed star of Inanna/Ishtar.

created by the union of fresh water—personified as the masculine Apsu—and salt water—the feminine Tiamat. Internecine conflict followed, and the god of the waters, Ea (the Sumerian Enki) murdered his father Apsu, thus enraging his mother, Tiamat, who created a host of monstrous serpents to help her avenge her consort's death. Marduk, however, defeated and dismembered her, creating the sky and world from parts of her body, and using the blood of her serpent son, Kingu, to create humanity. This myth is one of the first instances of a male god defeating his mother to assume a creator role for himself. Tiamat, like her Sumerian counterpart, Nammu, may be symbolized as a dragon, while her epic battle with Marduk inspired many subsequent heroic tales, including that of St. George and the dragon.

Following Sargon I of Agade's conquest of Babylonia, the golden age of Babylon gave way in turn to Assyrian rulership. The warlike Assyrians preserved the Sumerian/Babylonian pantheon, although Marduk was displaced in favor of the Assyrian national deity, Ashur. As befitted a people which had risen to prominence through warfare, Ishtar, often depicted standing on the back of a fierce lion as she led the Assyrians to victory, was especially venerated. Within Assyrian society, women were highly honored, for the right to kingship passed though the matriarchal line: thus the daughter of Sargon, Enheduanna, was exalted as the chief priestess, or "moon-minister to the Most High." It is through the vivid imagery of Enheduanna's poetry that we learn that Ishtar was revered as "a dragon, destroying by fire and flood...filling rivers with blood." Indeed, such was her importance that *ishtar* became a generic noun meaning "goddess."

Inanna/Ishtar was undoubtedly the most important Mesopotamian goddess, not only because she had survived the upheavals of Mesopotamian strife, but because she was strengthened in the process. She was represented in a number of forms, reflecting her multitude of roles. Sumerian images portrayed her as a winged figure who wore a horned crown at the center of which stood a cone, symbolizing the cosmic mountain. Among her most notable astral symbols were the eight-pointed star (sometimes represented as a rosette) that denoted the planet Venus; the lunar crescent in her aspect as daughter of the moon god; her rainbow necklace, whose seven colors may be equated to the seven gates of the underworld through which she passed; and her girdle, which was made up of the constellations of the zodiac. The lion that she dominated represented her war-loving aspect, as did the mace, spear, double-headed ax and bow that she brandished (which also symbolized the star Sirius, with which she was equated). As a fertility goddess, she was depicted by a full-bodied figurine, an echo of the ancient "Venus figures." In common with Ninhursag, the bountiful cow, or its lunar-shaped horns, were her attributes, while all vegetation was sacred to her, particularly corn and such trees as the fig, olive, date and apple, all of which represented the tree of life. When portrayed as a goddess of death, she was accompanied by serpents and dragons, or by a scorpion (also a form of Ishara, a sea goddess), both of which are dual lunar and fertility symbols.

Although the Sumerian, Babylonian and Assyrian pantheons are regarded as the most important expressions of Mesopotamian sacred belief, other civilizations, including those of the Hurrians and the Hittites, enjoyed rich cosmogonies and mythologies, many of which display syncretic influences. By about 2300 BC, the leading Hurrian goddess was Hebat, consort of Teschub (the weather god) and mother of Sharruma, whose primary attribute was the lion that was her mount. Despite the fact that Teschub had the power to bring rain, Hebat controlled the sun and moon, and was also venerated as the mistress of animals and patroness of the hunt. The goddess Shaushka, who may also be equated with Ishtar, shared this significance, as manifested by her wings and attendant lion. The Hittites (c. 1740–1460 BC), too, worshipped a sun goddess, Arinna, to whom they attributed sovereignty over both heaven and earth; in her manifestation as Hatti, the winged throne goddess, she lent her protection to the king; her "husband" was regarded as a more remote lord of the pantheon and dispenser of justice. The land of Elam (c. 2550–1860 BC) was considered even by its contemporaries as a law unto itself. Described as a realm of witches ruled by magic, the Elamites acknowledged as their supreme deity the mother goddess of the moon, who wielded powers of enchantment and death. She was represented in the form of female figurines, and although her primary symbol was the serpent, she was also depicted with the bull and ram—all of them implying her role as a bestower of fecundity.

THE WEST SEMITIC GODDESS

In common with Mesopotamia, the regions of Syria and Palestine were successively dominated by a series of civilizations centered loosely around city-states, many of which promoted their own deities, but which also preserved the pantheons that they had inherited from their predecessors. Furthermore, since these lands were a hub of trade, they were open to many external influences, including other systems of sacred belief, as seen in the many similarities between Mesopotamian goddesses and their West Semitic counterparts.

Of all these civilizations, the Canaanite was perhaps the most significant, for the deities of its pantheon—especially its goddesses—had a great influence over the sacred beliefs of the Aramaeans, Philistines and Phoenicians. Although male deities had nominal predominance over goddesses, as in the Mesopotamian myths, the multifaceted Goddess was of crucial, if not paramount, significance in maintaining the divine order. The head of the Canaanite family of gods was El, the elderly creator god and husband of Athirat (also known as Asherah or Elat); together this first couple gave life to all the other deities. The fact that this mother goddess was also known as Lady Athirat of the Sea testifies to the Goddess's association with water in her function as a demiurge. But in Athirat's case, rather than assuming the terrible characteristics of Tiamat (whose role was usurped here by the male sea god, Yam) she appears to have been an entirely benevolent goddess who used her beauty to intercede with her husband on behalf of her children—as, for instance, when Baal and Anat elicited her help in securing El's permission to build a palace. Among her leading symbols was the spindle, at which she worked peacefully by the sea, but of more profound importance was the tree of life, reflecting her role as the mother of more than seventy deities; in temples, an unhewn block of wood (itself termed an *asherah*) was used to signify her presence.

However, despite their major parental

Above: A stylized portrayal of the West Semitic Astarte (who was worshipped under the name of Tanit by the Phoenicians). Both her wings and the dove that she holds emphasize her heavenly power, as well as her patronage of love.

Background: A scorpion, attribute of Inanna/Ishtar as goddess of death.

Right:
The bull, epitomizing strength and virility, had powerful symbolism in Canaanite mythology. El, the supreme god, was called "the bull," while the union of Baal and Anat (described as "a heifer" in the Ras Shamra texts) resulted in the goddess giving birth to a bull, "his [father's] likeness."

Right: *The Canaanite Ras Shamra tells how Anat, determined to attain Aqhat's bow, instructed her servant Yatpan to transform herself into an eagle. In this form, she descended upon the unfortunate prince and killed him, winning the bow for her mistress.*

roles, El and Athirat were depicted as passive, distant figures in comparison to their children, the storm god Baal and his violent sister and consort Anat (or Anatha, Anath-Ma). The Canaanite Ras Shamra texts tell how, after having Baal subdue Yam, Anat stained her body with red henna, smeared her face with purple dye, and perfumed herself with the scent of coriander before laying frenzied waste to a terrestrial town: "Heads roll like balls beneath her. Hands fly like locusts above her.... She plunged her knees in the blood of the guards." After Baal was murdered by the god of death, Mot, thus bringing drought upon the world (a fate particularly dreaded in this desert region), she followed her brother/consort to the underworld, where "she seized Mot and split him with a sword. She burned him with fire and ground him with millstones. She scattered him in a field and the birds ate his flesh," thus restoring both Baal's life and the fertility of the earth. Anat clearly relished her role as a bringer of war and death, yet through her devotion to Baal, she was also a goddess of love and fertility. Her primary symbol is that of life itself—blood—and, in homage to Anat's blood lust, her worshippers, too, dyed themselves with henna. Another of her attributes was the bow that she stole from the prince Aqhat with the help of her attendant, Yatpan, who transformed herself into an eagle in order to wrest the weapon from the resistant mortal. Like most other fearsome goddesses of battle, Anat was represented in the company of a lion.

Despite the devotion that their followers accorded Athirat and Anat, it is another goddess—Astarte (or Ashtoreth)—who appears to have been the greatest object of adoration among the West Semitic goddesses, for not only was she venerated by

the Canaanites, but also by the Philistines and especially the Phoenicians (who, in Carthage, knew her as Tanit, the queen of heaven). Like Ishtar, with whom she is almost interchangeable, Astarte was a dual goddess of love and war. She was often represented in clay statuettes as a voluptuous figure, underlining her role as a promoter of fertility, and was sometimes depicted wearing a cow-horn headdress; symbols of fecundity like corn accompanied her image, as did lunar attributes like the dove or lily. As the queen of heaven, she was symbolized by the star and moon that were also sacred to Ishtar, or even by the ankh that was the attribute of Isis.

The "Syrian goddess," Atargatis, whose cult originated with the Aramaeans, combined the characteristics of Anat and Astarte. She was said to have been hatched from an egg that fell miraculously from the heavens, and was thus the queen of the waters, from which she created the cosmos. In recognition of her primary domain, Atargatis was often portrayed as a mermaidlike creature, sporting the tail of the fish that was sacred to her (and which her worshippers were forbidden to eat), in the company of fertility-bearing serpents. Such was the resonance of her power that her cult spread throughout the Greco-Roman world: the Roman emperor Nero paid her homage.

THE PHRYGIAN GODDESS

While Atargatis enjoyed a considerable following outside Syria, the most popular "foreign" goddess to be incorporated into Greco-Roman sacred beliefs was Cybele, the object of an intense and orgiastic mystery cult and originally the Phrygian mother of all living things. It is believed that her worship began in Anatolia around 1200 BC, but most of the information on her is derived from Greco-Roman sources, which, among other fascinating details, record that in 200 BC Celtic priests attended her festival in Anatolia. She was a significant deity in Greece before the black stone that embodied her presence was carried to Rome by order of the Cumaean Sibyl in 204 BC. Here she was accorded the supreme honor of having the first festival of the year—Megalensia, or Megalesia—dedicated to her, for as the *magna mater*, or great mother, she preceded all the deities whom she had created.

The black stone that signaled her presence in Rome was probably a meteorite, on which her image was said to be visible. In her Anatolian incarnation, she was portrayed as a lioness who wore a crenellated crown; among the Greco-Roman Cybele's symbols was the dove, whose form she could assume; it also served as her messenger. However, most of Cybele's symbolic attributes were associated with the myths about her relationship with her young lover, Attis, which parallel the stories of Inanna/Ishtar and Dumuzi/Tammuz. Attis himself was of miraculous birth, for he was said to have been conceived—possibly by Cybele herself—from an almond (a feminine sexual symbol). His beauty was such that Cybele fell in love with him and claimed him for her own. When he enjoyed a dalliance with the nymph Sagaritis, Cybele's jealous rage drove Attis mad, and he castrated himself. To prevent him from taking his own life,

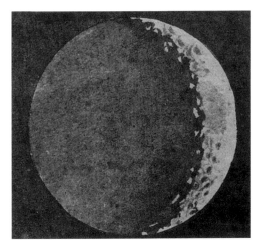

Cybele transformed him into a pine—a tree that then became sacred to her. Other versions of the myth relate that Cybele married Attis against her father's wishes, thus provoking her parent to kill her lover; or that Attis was castrated by an amorous Phrygian king. Thus, to men, Cybele was a terrifying, yet fascinating, mother goddess of rampant sexuality, who, if crossed, had the power of emasculation. Indeed, the male priests of her cult castrated themselves in her service, a practice that outraged the predominantly masculine Roman society. Her cult was officially banned until the late first century AD.

Reflecting her Near Eastern origins, Cybele was often depicted in a chariot drawn by lions; she could also be represented by the Goddess's crescent moon, or by the musical instruments that accompanied her veneration. At the culmination of their wild rituals, her worshippers bathed in the blood of a freshly sacrificed bull (*taurobolium*), the bull representing the male fertility principle that must lay down its life for the mother goddess, and the baptism of blood, the gift of rebirth that lay within her power. Perhaps her most profound symbol, immortalized in her name (which may be translated as "cavern-dweller"), was the cave, testifying to her ancient origins as the goddess from whose primeval womb all life had sprung.

Left: As in many other systems of sacred belief, the moon was a profoundly symbolic attribute of many important Near Eastern mother goddesses, including Cybele. Its cycle of waxing and waning was identified with the Goddess's unrivaled powers over birth, death and regeneration.

The Goddess in Mediterranean Civilizations

It is a remarkable tribute to the power of the mythologies of the early Mediterranean civilizations—most notably those of ancient Egypt, Greece and Rome—that we remain familiar with the names and characteristics of their leading deities thousands of years after the decline of their active worship. This is due partly to the rich legacy of documentation and vivid pictorial images that has survived (which also tells us about the symbolism associated with each deity), but it also reflects the enduring fascination of colorful, immortal lives. The sacred beliefs that collectively dominated the Mediterranean region were characterized by enormous pantheons of deities, which were generally led by a male god. Yet despite her apparent subjugation to the masculine principle, the Goddess continued to play a vitally important role as creator, mother and preserver of the natural order of life and death, the devotion that she inspired in her various incarnations making her the subject of more intense, personal worship than most male gods enjoyed. And, because of the syncretic nature of these essentially pragmatic beliefs, veneration of such goddesses as Isis spread far beyond the bounds of their original areas of worship, illustrating the Goddess's enduring ability to awe and inspire.

THE EGYPTIAN GODDESS

Although, as elsewhere, a vast number of lesser deities—each of which protected the particular locality with which its veneration was associated—figured prominently in the sacred beliefs of ancient Egypt, during the period of the Old Kingdom (c. 2686–2181 BC) a pantheon of nine "state" gods whose worship became general emerged. Known collectively as the

Opposite: Isis and her brother/consort Osiris.
Below: *Isis kneels on the hieroglyphic signifying gold, holding the* shen *ring that represents eternity.*
Background: *The ankh.*

ennead, this divine family comprised the sun and creator god Re (also called Atum or, in Thebes, Amum); his children, Shu (god of the air) and Tefnut (goddess of moisture, dew and rain); Shu and Tefnut's offspring, Geb (the earth god) and Nut (goddess of the sky); and Geb and Nut's children, the male deities Osiris and Set, and the goddesses Isis and Nephtys.

Worship of this ennead centered on the city of Heliopolis, which, according to its priests, was the site of the cosmic mountain (which it is possible that the pyramids were built to symbolize) that emerged from the primeval waters of Nun. (Unusually, Nun was generally personified as a masculine deity, yet some traditions told that Nun formed a cosmic partnership with the goddess Nunet.) Here, it was said, Re willed himself into existence, and then single-handedly brought Shu and Tefnut into being. Thus it may appear that the procreative powers of the Goddess were dispensed with in the Heliopolitan cosmogony, but it should be remembered that while the heat of the sun that beat relentlessly on the Egyptian earth was so great that it was most readily identifiable with masculine strength, it was the goddess Tefnut who represented the relief brought to the arid land by the moisture that she embodied. Yet despite her aqueous associations, which may be depicted by her jar of life-giving water, her symbolism primarily proclaims her status as the daughter of the sun god, for she was personified as having the head of a lion (a solar attribute) and wearing the solar disk (which some also associate with the world egg) as a crown.

Through the union of Tefnut and Shu, Geb and Nut were born. Again, it is relatively rare that the deity of the earth should be regarded as a male, but this discrepancy was perhaps counterbalanced by the fact that it was Nut who was most frequently depicted in Egyptian art, and who was the object of a more devoted following than her brother/consort. It was said that after she had given birth to Osiris, Set, Isis and Nephtys, she was raised to the sky by Re, her body thus forming the vault of the heavens over which Re sprinkled the stars (hence her appellation "starry one"). She was most often depicted in this athletic, arched stance, with Shu, her father, supporting and separating her body from Geb, and with the Milky Way—representing the milk that she produced as the celestial cow—adorning her torso. Because some believed that she swallowed the sun each night and gave it new life each morning, she was also termed "mother of the sun." Additionally, she was regarded as the protectress of the dead (perhaps because Re's solar boat was believed to sail through the underworld at night), and her image was painted on the inner lids of sarcophagi, which may also have symbolized the return of the dead to the womb of the Goddess.

While Nut and Tefnut figured prominently in the Heliopolitan cosmogony, it was Nut's daughter, Isis, who was recognized as the most powerful goddess. It was told that the evil Set murdered his brother Osiris, and, after placing his body in a casket, floated it down the Nile. The distraught Isis eventually recovered the corpse of her brother/husband from

Byblos, but Set discovered and dismembered it, scattering its parts all over Egypt. With the help of Thoth, the god of wisdom and the moon, who tutored her in magical powers, Isis assumed the shape of a kite and flew ceaselessly over the land until she had eventually located all of Osiris's body parts. She reassembled them with the help of her sister, Nephtys, as well as Nephtys's son by Osiris, Anubis, the jackal-headed god of embalming. By fanning his body with her kite's wings, Isis resurrected Osiris just long enough to conceive a son, Horus. Having thus demonstrated her qualities as an exemplary wife, Isis now dedicated her formidable energies to protecting her son against Set. When grown, Horus avenged his father's murder in battle, after which Osiris became the ruler of the underworld and judge of the dead, and Horus the lord of the sky.

It was as the devoted mother of Horus, who was regarded as the mythical ancestor of the pharaohs, that Isis was especially celebrated, and numerous depictions showed her tenderly nursing her son in her lap (an archetypal image that was

Left: Many Egyptian goddesses, including Bast, Ubastet and Pakhit, were associated with felines like the panther, representing both their ferocious and sensual aspects. **Opposite, top:** *Isis extends the kite's wings with which she flew in search of Osiris' dismembered body, and which empowered her to fan the breath of life.* **Opposite, below:** *Isis and Nephtys, wearing throne and house headdresses respectively, encourage the sun to rise from the djed pillar that represents Osiris's spine. An armed ankh holds aloft the solar disk, venerated by baboons.* **Below:** *Some historians believe that the Egyptian pyramids symbolize the cosmic mountain, which the hybrid sphinx guards vigilantly, recalling the determination and strength with which Isis protected Horus.* **Background:** *Stars symbolizing the goddess Nut.*

Right: A Greco-Roman depiction of a many-breasted Isis, signifying her powers of nourishment as a mother goddess, surrounded by the various creatures of land, sea and air that symbolize her mastery over the natural world.

Right: This sculpture (c. 1400 BC) represents the fearsome lion-headed Sekhmet, whose symbolism identifies her as a war goddess.

later applied to the Christian Madonna and the infant Jesus). In reflection of her maternal role, Isis was also symbolically personified as a white sow or cow (whose head, some said, Thoth gave her after Horus decapitated her in his anger that she had shown mercy to Set after his defeat). She was also depicted bearing the solar disk between her cow-horn headdress. Because she had resurrected Osiris from the dead, she was accorded such life-giving symbols as the basket within which

she placed Osiris's body parts, the grain whose growth represented Osiris's resurrection, or a jar from which, like Tefnut, she poured water on the land; indeed, the tears that she shed on Osiris's death were said to cause the annual flooding of the Nile. She was also sometimes shown wearing the vulture headdress, which represented her function as bearer of the dead, and also—through the bird's habit of scavenging—purification. In this headdress, the vulture was frequently combined with the uraeus, the rearing form of a cobra, a dual symbol of rebirth and protection. Her importance as Osiris's consort was underlined by the ankh that she sometimes carried—a complex symbol of life that unites the tau cross that represents Osiris, and the oval (an ideogram for the womb) of Isis, and which has been interpreted as the key to eternal life. As consort of the lord of the underworld, she was represented crowned with a throne (the hieroglyph of her name) at the side of her husband, or in association with the crescent moon (also a symbol of the great mother).

The worship of Nephtys was in some instances combined with that of Isis, for the two exhibited remarkable sisterly solidarity: even though Set was Nephtys's husband, it was she who helped her sister reassemble and embalm Osiris's body and

who supported her throughout her grief. She was regarded as Isis's darker side, yet this association was not by any means negative, for she too was perceived as a benevolent protector of the dead, and was thus, like Isis and many other Egyptian goddesses, symbolized by the vulture, as well as by her primary attribute, the moon. While Isis wore the throne hieroglyph as a headdress, Nephtys was crowned with the hieroglyph that denoted a house—symbolizing both the divine pantheon and the ancestral dynasty of the pharaohs.

Ma'at, goddess of truth, whose responsibility was maintaining divine order, was another deity with strong connections to the underworld, for she played a crucial role in the judgement of the souls of those who had recently died. In Osiris's hall of judgement, the heart of the deceased would be weighed against the ostrich feather that symbolized truth, and which also personified the goddess herself. "Make me light," prayed the Egyptians, for if their hearts outweighed her feather, they would be condemned to the terrible jaws of the crocodilelike monster Ammit, and thus to eternal death.

If female members of the ennead were the most closely connected with cosmic functions in the Heliopolitan mythologies, there were also many other goddesses who were significant objects of veneration in ancient Egypt. One of the most important was Hathor, a deity of ancient origin who became closely associated with Isis during the period of the New Kingdom (c. 1567–1085 BC). She too was worshipped as a great mother and depicted as the celestial cow, who was often represented suckling the infant pharaoh. The solar disk that she bore between her horns has particular significance in this context, for she was sometimes termed "the golden egg of the sun," or "the Nile Goose" who laid the cosmic egg. Hathor was also identified with Tefnut, for it was told that the latter once

abandoned Egypt for Nubia: persuaded to return, she reappeared in the form of Hathor. This occasioned such joy among the other gods that Re set her upon his forehead in the form of the uraeus—the cobra equated with the "eye of Re." Hathor could also assume Nut's attributes, for her body was sometimes represented as spangled with stars, and the Milky Way was said to flow from her breasts. She was also envisaged in a sevenfold form, as the Hathors—protectresses of newborn children and nourishers of the deceased. In common with other Egyptian mother goddesses, Hathor's attributes included many symbols of natural abundance, including the lotus (from which some believed the universe emerged) and the sycamore tree, which the ancient Egyptians venerated as the tree of life on account of the milky sap that it produces.

A multitude of lesser goddesses were also venerated as maternal deities, many of whom assumed part-animal form. Heket, for example, the consort of the Nile god Khnemu, was symbolized by the fecund frog, while Renenet was said to

Above and below: Both the mother goddess Isis (below) and Hathor (above) were portrayed with the head or headdress of the nurturing cow.
Background: *The goddess Nekhebet.*

assume the form of a lioness, and Nekhebet that of a vulture, when suckling their young. Nekhebet was sometimes worshipped in conjunction with her sister, Uadjet, the serpent mother of the Nile Delta, whose primary symbols included the serpent and uraeus. Tauert, too, was a widely venerated Nile mother goddess, represented as a hippopotamus. Yet despite the host of mother goddesses, there were those who had more sinister functions: Sekhmet, for instance, was a fearsome war goddess personified as a mighty lioness. Although she too had a martial aspect, the moon goddess Bastet, whose cult centered on Bubastis, was an ambiguous deity, for she was also celebrated as a goddess of pleasure. She was represented in the form of the cat, whose characteristics are similarly ambivalent, an association underlined by the fact that the dilation of feline

pupils appears to mimic the waxing and waning of the moon.

Yet despite this abundance of goddesses, it was Isis alone, as "she of a thousand names," who reconciled all the more specific attributes of her divine sisters within herself. In reflection of her profound importance to her worshippers, Lucius Apuleius, an adherent of Isis's mystery cult in Rome, recorded the words that she spoke to him in *The Golden Ass*: "I am Nature, the universal Mother, mistress of all the elements, primordial child of time, sovereign of all things spiritual, queen of the dead, queen also of the immortals, the single manifestation of all gods and goddesses that are." Wife, mother, and mistress of the magical powers of regeneration, she was worshipped for more than 3,000 years in Egypt, Greece and Rome.

These pages:
*Representations of Egyptian nobles, including Pharaoh Akenaten's wife Nefertiti (opposite, below), a noblewoman with slaves (opposite, top right) and the richly dressed bearers of offerings (above), are similar to the portrayals of deities and incorporate sacred symbolism. The pharaoh was believed to be a reincarnation of the divine Horus. At left is Bastet, the moon goddess, symbolized by the sacred cat. **Background:** Isis nursing Horus.*

Right: Detail from a painted Greek vase (c. 560–525 BC) representing the terrible Gorgon Medusa, her head wreathed with snakes, whose gaze turned one to stone. After Perseus killed her, Medusa's head was placed at the center of Athena's shield.

THE GRECO-ROMAN GODDESS

Archaeological evidence attests to a significant Goddess cult in both the Minoan civilization (c. 3000–1000 BC) of Crete and the Mycenaean society (c. 1600–1400 BC) of Greece, which imported many Minoan sacred concepts. Minoan seals symbolize the "mistress of the animals" in their depictions of the Goddess standing atop a mound (possibly the cosmic mountain), in the company of such animals as lions, bulls or rams—all attributes of fecund strength. Statuettes gave her a bell-shaped lower torso (symbolic of the womb) and a snake-entwined body, emphasizing her role as a bringer of fertility. Further symbols associated with this early goddess were the double ax, which, in the hands of a male deity, represented the thunderbolt, but which in the Goddess context suggests the butterfly that is "reborn" from a caterpillar into a glorious, winged creature, as well as the crescent-shaped bull's horns that indicate a lunar, as well as a sacrificial, association. Although some aspects of the early Minoan/Mycenaean Goddess survived, the sophisticated system of sacred belief that later evolved in Greece was based on a cosmogony and pantheon of gods that exhibited remarkable similarities to those of the Egyptian Heliopolis. And after their contact with the Greek civilization, the admiring Romans—who had previously worshiped local deities—adopted the Greek pantheon virtually wholesale (while Latinizing the names of the deities). They justified their actions on the basis that all deities were universal, merely addressed by different names.

Despite the number of often conflicting Greek myths, it was Hesiod, writing in the eighth or seventh century BC, who first recorded the theogonies ("birth of the gods") that personified creation and the forces of nature as deities. In the beginning, he said, there was the primeval vacuum, Chaos, whom Hesiod regarded as female. From Chaos's womb emerged Gaia (also called Ge), goddess of the earth, and then Eros, god of love, closely followed by the goddess Nyx (the deity of the night, personified with black wings and wearing a dark robe studded with stars) and her brother Erebus (darkness), the pair who brought day and space into being. Gaia alone created the sea, Pontus, and then Ouranos, god of the sky, whom she took as her husband, giving birth as a result to many children, including the Titans. However, Ouranos banished his children to the depths of the earth, and the enraged Gaia incited her Titan son Kronos to emasculate him with a sickle, thus separating the earth from the sky. Kronos then assumed leadership of the gods. Gaia's insatiable sexual appetite is apparent in the huge numbers of children she bore. She was credited with powers of prophecy, and the oracle at Delphi (whose name is derived from the Greek word for womb), which was guarded by her python son, was originally hers. It passed successively to Themis, Phoebe and, finally, Apollon. Known as *tellus mater* in Rome, Gaia was the great mother *par excellence*, and her attributes include all the symbols of natural abundance sacred to so many other earth goddesses, but she was also specifically associated with the agricultural sickle (whose shape resembles that of the crescent moon), and the serpent, a universal feminine symbol of fertility.

The Titan goddesses inherited and propagated their mother's creative functions. Theia, goddess of light and sister/wife of Hyperion, gave birth to the god Helios (the sun), Selene (goddess of the moon), and Eos (dawn). Themis, the guardian of the law whose symbol was a pair of scales, was said to have been a wife of Zeus and mother of the Horae, Eunomia, Dice, Eirene, Astraea, the three Moirae and also of the Hesperides. Mnemosyne, too, took Zeus as her husband, their union producing the nine Muses. Phoebe mated with her brother Coeus, by whom she had Asteria (also the name of the island subsequently called Delos, into which she transformed herself) and Leto. With her brother/consort Oceanus, Tethys was the ruler of the sea and mother of the

innumerable river deities, collectively termed the Oceanides. Rhea mated with Kronos, and gave birth to Hestia, Demeter, Hera, Hades and Poseidon, all of whom Kronos, terrified that he would be dethroned by his children just as he had overthrown his father, swallowed at birth. However, Rhea was able to save Zeus, who grew up to successfully challenge his father with the help of his regurgitated siblings and thus became the head of the family of deities who lived on Mount Olympus (of which Gaia, as Gaia Olympia, was mother). The identity of Rhea as a mother goddess was often fused with that of Gaia (whose scythe she carried as Rhea Kronia, and whose adjunctive name, "Pandora," and sacred vase, she shared). Rhea was also identified with Demeter (whom she became, according to some myths), and also with Cybele, who, like Rhea, was frequently depicted riding in a chariot drawn by lions.

The twelve Olympians became the greatest Greco-Roman deities and the objects of universal worship. They included the gods Zeus (the Roman Jupiter), Poseidon (Neptune), Helios or Apollon (Apollo), Ares (Mars), Hermes (the swift Mercury), Hephaestos (Vulcan), and the major goddesses Hera (Juno), Athena (wise Minerva), Aphrodite (Venus), Artemis (Diana),

Above: The Delphic Oracle was the outlet for the prophetic voices of Gaia and her Titan daughters before it was usurped by Apollon, who replaced Gaia's python guardian with his own priestess, the Pythia or "Pythoness."

Left and opposite, below: These Mycenaean Goddess figurines date from about 1400–1200 BC. The figure opposite derives her pointed facial features from an even more ancient archetype, that of the bird goddess, whose wings have evolved into upraised arms, signifying epiphany. The face of the figure at left resembles that of a sow, a creature that was also equated with the Goddess.

Background: The hybrid sphinx.

Right: The Titan Rhea, daughter of the earth goddess Gaia and mother of the Olympian deities Zeus, Hera, Hades, Poseidon, Demeter and Hestia, was widely venerated as a powerful mother goddess.

Below: The scenes of warfare vibrantly depicted on this black-figured amphora show why the ancient Greeks venerated such goddesses as Athena for their martial qualities.

Background: Demeter, Greek goddess of agriculture.

Demeter (Ceres), and Hestia (Vesta). As Zeus's sister/wife, Hera was the Olympian "first lady," regarded as the protector of women, goddess of marriage, and a maternal deity in her capacity as the mother of Ares, Hebe (the goddess of youth and cupbearer of the Olympians), Hephaestos, Eileithyia (goddess of birth), and Eris (goddess of discord). The nurturing cow, many-seeded pomegranate and cornucopia of abundance were among her primary symbols, as was the lily with which she was said to have conceived Ares. Although the cuckoo, in whose form Zeus nestled within her breast during their early period of courtship, was sacred to her, perhaps the bird that best personified Hera was the peacock—the symbol of pride. For not only was she constantly consumed with jealousy at Zeus's philandering (frequently with doleful results for his paramours), she created the stately bird from the corpse of the giant Argus, setting his hundred eyes in its tail.

Hera's sister, Demeter, shared much of her symbolism as a mother goddess. She, too, was represented by the cow and the cornucopia, but also by the pig and grain, for her domain was that of agriculture and the earth. Indeed, her crucial role in the regulation of agriculture was embodied in the poignant tale of the temporary loss of her daughter, re-enacted annually by members of the Eleusinian mystery cult (whose symbol was a sheaf of corn). It was believed that Demeter's adored daughter, Persephone (or Kore, "maiden"), was gathering flowers when Hades, god of the underworld, saw and desired her, and abducted her to his shadowy kingdom. Demeter was maddened by grief and withdrew her gift of fertility from the earth, bringing drought and famine wherever she wandered before she finally reached Eleusis. Eventually, Zeus interceded and agreed to restore Demeter's daughter to the earth, but because Persephone had eaten the seeds of a pomegranate (her symbol) while in the underworld, she was compelled to spend part of the year with Hades. This provided an explanation for the agricultural "death" heralded by the winter season, and the "rebirth" of nature in spring. Despite her primary association with natural fertility, Demeter was also regarded as a goddess of death, for she transformed her mortal lover, Mecon, into a poppy—a flower that became sacred to her. However, it was Persephone, by virtue of the period that she spent in the underworld, who was more closely associated with death. Along with the pomegranate, her symbolic attributes were the keys to the underworld and the mint plant into which she and her mother transformed the nymph Mintha, the clandestine lover of the dreaded Hades.

Perhaps more than that of any other Greek goddess, the mythological lineage of Artemis can be traced directly back to the ancient "mistress of the animals" depicted on the Minoan seals. There is some conflict as to her parentage, but the prevailing belief was probably that she was the daughter of Zeus and Leto, who escaped Hera's wrath and gave birth to the

that these are not breasts, but rather fruit, or even bulls' testicles: whichever is correct, all are fertility symbols. This depiction of Artemis as a mother goddess was compounded by her function as the deity of childbirth, for it was said that, as the first-born, she had helped Leto to deliver Apollon. In common with many other such goddesses, including Demeter and Athena, Artemis could be represented by the (queen) bee, who was served by female *melissae* (bees) and castrated male *essenes* (drones). Her other attributes included fish (through her lunar association) and

Left: The peacock was sacred to Hera, who set the hundred eyes of the fallen giant Argus into the bird's tail. The "eyes" symbolized Hera's all-seeing powers.
Below: *Primavera, the Roman personification of spring, tends the shrubs that herald nature's annual awakening.*
Background: *The poppy, symbol of Demeter.*

twins Artemis (goddess of the moon) and Apollon (god of the sun). Thus the crescent moon (and the scythe) were Artemis's primary symbols. Because she was also regarded as the goddess of wild animals, who both protected them and assisted their human hunters, her other important attributes were the bow (curved, like the crescent moon), the arrow (symbolizing illumination), and such game animals as the stag (into which she transformed Actaeon), boar (whose killers she punished) and bear (the form into which Zeus changed her companion Callisto). Also sacred to her were the dogs (ancient symbols of healing) trained for the hunt. As the lunar huntress, she was a virginal, vengeful figure, yet identification with the objects of other Goddess cults sometimes credited her with more benevolent characteristics. As Diana of Ephesus, for example, whose temple was counted among one of the seven wonders of the classical world, she was sculpted as an elegant figure from whose form many breastlike orbs were suspended. Some interpreters have claimed

Right: The rose was among
the primary attributes
of Aphrodite, the Greek
goddess of love; the flower's
beauty and fragrance
evoked the loveliness and
sensuality of this deity
and came to represent
love itself.

the fir tree (as an evergreen, a symbol of
immortality), in whose groves she liked to
roam. In reconciling all these apparently
conflicting characteristics and functions,
Artemis was truly the heiress to the ancient
earth-mother tradition.

If Artemis was an ambivalent goddess,
whom some of her worshippers attempted
to placate by sacrifice, Aphrodite was the
straightforward deity of love, beauty and
sexual pleasure, whose worship many
scholars believe derived from that of
Astarte. Some myths said that she was created from the severed genitals of Ouranos
that fell into the sea—she floated ashore
as the "sea-foam-born" goddess; others,
that she was a daughter of Zeus by Dione.
The former, more colorful version, cap-
tured the popular imagination, and thus
she was known as Aphrodite Urania
(depicted astride a sea goose or swan) or
Aphrodite Marina ("of the sea"), shown
with the attributes of the pearl and scallop shell. All of these evoke the Goddess
in her aqueous, lunar aspect, as do the fish,
the fecund turtle and the dolphin, called
"the woman of the sea," whose name

derives from the Greek for "womb".
Although married to the unattractive
Hephaestos, Aphrodite led a promiscuous
immortal life, her favored lover being Ares,
god of war—her partiality perhaps
demonstrating the unfathomable influence of sexual chemistry. She had the
power, which she often used mischievously,
to make the most unlikely love matches,

Right: Fragonard's
eighteenth-century
portrayal of a languorous
Diana (Artemis) reflects
the ambiguity of the lunar
goddess's dual role as
virgin deity of the hunt
and the mother goddess
who presided over child-
birth. Three of Diana's
symbols appear here:
the crescent moon behind
the reclining goddess; the
animal skin in which she
is draped; and the quiver
of arrows that lies within
her reach.

often aided by her magical girdle of infatuation. Notoriously (although justifiably) vain, one of her major attributes was the mirror with which she admired herself (from which are derived the modern botanical and zoological symbol of femininity). The planet Venus—the Morning Star—was named in her honor. Her multitude of natural symbols—primarily the rose and dove, but also the myrtle and swallow, as well as the violets that garlanded her head—are mainly those that were admired for their beauty and that came to symbolize love. But the red apple testifies to her vanity, for it was awarded her by Paris (thus slighting Hera and Athena) as the fairest goddess of them all, which led ultimately to the Trojan War.

In contrast with Aphrodite's carnality, Athena, the goddess of reason, learning and crafts, yet also of war, was venerated for her cerebral qualities. One of the myths of her birth tells how after Athena was conceived by her Oceanides mother, Metis ("wisdom"), the first wife of Zeus, he—perhaps sensibly, given the Olympian family history—feared that the unborn child

Left: A detail from Botticelli's The Birth of Venus *(c. 1483–84) portrays the beautiful Venus (Aphrodite) blown ashore by the winds on a scallop shell (one of her leading symbols).*

Background: The scallop shell of Venus (Aphrodite).

would overthrow him, and so swallowed Metis. It is said that Athena subsequently sprang fully formed from his head, dressed and armed as a warrior. In her martial aspect she was symbolized by her spear, helmet (symbolizing thought) and shield, the *aegis*, which conferred divine protection—indeed, Athena was usually considered a defensive rather than an

Below: Alexandre Cabanel's painting The Birth of Venus *(1863) illustrates the moment of the goddess's divine incarnation, celebrated ecstatically by the cherubic attendants with which she became associated.*

Right: Athena in martial regalia, her helmet, spear and aegis *representing her warlike aspect, with serpent from the ancient Minoan and Mycenaean Goddess. Background: The owl of Athena.*

aggressive goddess. Together, Athena's spear and *aegis* represented *epheboi*, or adulthood, in Greek society. The *aegis*, whose frame was crafted by Hephaestos and which was covered with the skin of the fairy she-goat Amalthea, which had once suckled Zeus, was originally the supreme god's property. When carried by Athena, it was emblazoned with the head of Medusa, which Perseus presented to her after he had decapitated the Gorgon, using the shield as a mirror to avoid Medusa's petrifying glare. Confusingly, the *aegis* was also referred to as the serpent-fringed cloak that Athena sometimes wore, the snake associating her with the Minoan and the Mycenaean Goddess. Perhaps the most popular of Athena's attributes was the owl (which abounded in her city, Athens): wisdom was ascribed to it through its ability to see in the dark, in symbolic terms, penetrating the murky depths of ignorance. In an interesting parallel with many warlike Celtic goddesses, Athena was sometimes associated with another bird, the black crow, a creature of ill omen that was said to scavenge corpses on battlefields. The olive was sacred to Athena, for it was said that she bestowed the first tree on the citizens of Athens, who thankfully made her their patron; when burned, its oil produced light, which aided study. Athena also gave humanity various agricultural implements, including the plow, and helped master the horse by means of the bridle and chariot. She furthermore taught women such useful crafts as weaving, and the renowned statue of Athena (now lost), called the Palladium (which was originally created in the image of her companion, Pallas, whom she had accidentally slain)

depicted the goddess clasping a distaff and spindle, as well as a spear.

The least well known of the Olympian goddesses was Hestia, who was forced to cede her position as the twelfth Olympian to Dionysos (Bacchus) after the fifth century BC. She was regarded as the keeper of the flame that burned on the Olympian hearth, and was thus the guardian of harmonious family life. Her protective function assumed a civic aspect, and in most towns her image was placed in the temple—called the Prytanitis—dedicated to her, in conjunction with her perpetually burning flame, a symbol of harmony, continuity and life. As the Roman Vesta, this goddess was similarly regarded as the protector of the public "hearth," whose symbolic fire was tended in her temple by the six vestal virgins—for she, too, had sworn to preserve her chastity.

These were the most important Greco-Roman goddesses, but others too numerous to describe were also worshipped. Some were inseparable from the natural phenomena that symbolized them, such as

linked with goddesses from other traditions. They include Maia, the mother of Hermes, who may be loosely associated by virtue of her miraculous motherhood with both Buddha and Christ's mothers; and Arachne, who challenged Athena to a weaving contest, lost, and was transformed into a spider whom, some said, spun the web of fate. However, this function was more frequently accorded to the Moirai (the Roman Parcae)—Nona ("nine"), Decima ("ten") and Morta "death")—who were said to live in a cave next to the sacred stream of immortality. Lachesis ("disposer of the lots") measured out the thread of each individual's life, Klotho ("the spinner") spun the thread, and Atropos ("the inflexible") severed it with her enormous deadly shears. Like the Fates of many other traditions, the primary symbols of this trio were thread, spinning, and shears (representing the creation, course and culmination of mortal life) and the web of destiny.

Selene, goddess of the moon, or Iris, the rainbow goddess and messenger of the gods. Others were more complex entities: Hecate, for example, was the goddess of magic, the crossroads, death and the lunar underworld. She was symbolized by the black dogs which accompanied her and which signaled their devotion by howling at the moon, and by the torches that she bore to light her way (symbols of intuition and enlightenment). Like the Celtic goddesses in whom such triplicity was further developed, Hecate was sometimes depicted with three heads, representing the various characteristics that she embodied. In a reversed context, the three Erinyes, or Furies (who were also hopefully termed the Eumenides, or "kindly ones," in an attempt to curry their favor), who were conceived of as black-skinned bitches, could be invoked as a single entity. Called Tisiphone ("retaliation") Megaera ("grudge") and Alecto ("unnameable"), they lived in the underworld, but emerged to wreak punishment. Several other female deities deserve mention because they are strongly

Opposite, below: The Venus de Milo. **Left:** *Worn out by her work for the jealous Aphrodite, Psyche fell into a deathlike coma, but was revived and made immortal by Zeus and then married Eros. Psyche's name is Greek for "the soul"; she symbolizes the human personality.* **Below:** *Raphael's portrayal of the three Graces: Aglaea ("radiance"), Thalia ("revelry") and Euphrosyne ("mirth"). Favored companions of Aphrodite, they hold the apples that show their link to the goddess.* **Background:** *The spider, named for Arachne.*

Germano-Norse, Celtic and Northern European Civilizations

I n common with those of the Mediterranean region, the earliest recorded mythologies of northern Europe were "peopled" with complex divine families whose members, through their interrelationship and actions, were believed to affect the cosmos and the terrestrial world directly. There are close parallels among all of these traditions, reflecting not only the archetypal pattern of their mythologies, but also the adoption of many features of Mediterranean sacred beliefs imported as their bearers moved northward. Yet although the northern goddesses may be associated with Mediterranean counterparts, they were credited with powers and characteristics that mirrored the specific concerns (such as martial success) of those who venerated them. For example, although she shared their crowlike attribute, Athena was never represented as so vicious a battle goddess as the triple Morrigan of Irish lore. Neither did the Mediterranean Goddess exert such a profoundly mystical influence on the collective human psyche as the Celtic goddess, whose sacred communion with the land and inseparable union with nature were at the core of her worshippers' beliefs and rituals. Indeed, she survived in the form of many female Christian saints even after the patriarchal, monotheistic Christian religion had imposed itself upon northern Europe, thus satisfying an enduring, primal human need that the Goddess alone could fulfill.

THE GERMANO-NORSE GODDESS

Although they would be influenced by Celts who swept eastward from the region that is now the Czech Republic, the original sacred beliefs of the Germanic people have been closely equated with those that were expressed more completely in the ninth-century AD poetry and thirteenth-century prose tales that comprise the Norse Edda (the Norse word for "great-grandmother"). Scandinavia was converted to Christianity in the tenth century, which perhaps accounts for the lesser prominence accorded the Germano-Norse goddesses than the gods by the Edda, and also the fact that Ragnorak, the cosmic battle that ends the rule of the gods, so resembles the Christian Apocalypse. Despite this syncretic qualification, as well as the fact that

Opposite: A romanticized Victorian portrait of Queen Guinevere, whose legendary beauty ultimately brought about King Arthur's fall. She is surrounded by the traditional attributes of such goddesses of love as Aphrodite (Venus), including the dove, rose and lily. **Below:** *The three Norns replenish the well of Urdrbrunnen, the water of life. In the background is the tree of life, Yggdrasil, surmounted by its eagle, while the four stags of the cardinal directions nibble at its leaves.* **Background:** *The ever-growing Tree of Life.*

Right: Freyja played a complex role in Germano-Norse belief, for she possessed powers of both fertility and combat. She is seen here in her martial aspect, symbolized by military accouterments, with her feline chariot pullers. Below: Rackham's brooding representation of Erda, the Germanic earth goddess (who is also equated with Berchta or Holda). Her name endures in the German word for earth, Erde. *Background: The swan, an emblem of the Norns.*

many aspects inherent in this mythology are derived from Greco-Roman sources, the picture emerges of a distinctly northern European system of sacred belief, in which the Goddess played a vital role.

The Norse cosmic world was centered on Yggdrasil, the sacred ash tree (an evergreen, which symbolized immortality). It was both an *axis mundi* and the supporter of all life forms within the nine worlds that nestled in its mighty branches and roots, including Asgard, the fortress of the gods; Vanaheim, the region of the fertility spirits; Midgard, the realm of humans; and Jotunheim, the land of the hostile frost giants. An eagle (a masculine, solar symbol) sat atop Yggdrasil, while the worm or dragon Nidhogg (a feminine, lunar creature) nibbled at its roots, the pair encouraged in their enmity by the mischievous squirrel Ratatosk, who scurried between them. Four stags (possibly representing the cardinal directions) were also believed to feed off Yggdrasil's bark, representing the stimulus of renewal by death.

One of the tree's three roots led to heaven, where the Norse Fates (Norns or Nornir), named Urdr ("earth," but also "past"), Verthandi ("present"), and Skuld ("future"), lived in a cave (a symbol of the womb). The trio were also known in early England as the Wyrd or Weird (Anglo-Saxon for Urdr) Sisters, who were subsequently immortalized in Shakespeare's *Macbeth*. Like their Greco-Roman counterparts, the Norns were envisaged as tending the sacred well of the water of life (Urdrbrunnen) that flowed through heaven, which was said to produce the "honeydew" that nourished the bees, and from which emerged the first pair of swans (feminine water birds). The Norns, too, spun and ultimately cut the thread of life, and were symbolized by the spindle or distaff, and by the moon and well from which the water of immortality was drawn. Regarded as more powerful than any other entities—including the gods, who could not alter the destiny that the three maidens controlled—the Norns also played a crucial role in the preservation of the cosmos, as symbolized by Yggdrasil, for each day

they applied a paste (made from the sacred water and the clay of its banks) to the tree's roots, thus providing it with sustenance and protecting it from drought.

Within the various worlds harbored by the Norse tree of life, a rich and often humorous mythological drama was played out. The Edda asserts that Allfather was the primal creator (reflecting the fact that these tales were recorded after northern Europe had been exposed to Christianity) and that Ymir, the ancestor of the frost giants, was the first (male) creature. Despite this emphasis, it was a feminine entity—the primeval cow Audumla ("nourisher" or "creator of the earth")—that provided. She fed Ymir with her milk, and gave life to Buri, the ancestor of the Aesir (gods), by licking away the salty ice that surrounded him until he emerged from his freezing prison. Buri's grandson, Odin, who would later dismember Ymir and thus create the human world, became the supreme Norse deity, the father of the pantheon of gods, whose wife was variously called Jorth ("earth," often linked with the goddess of the cosmic mountain, Frigg Fiörgynn) or Frigg. Jorth was also called the wife of Djevs (whose name shares the same root as that of Zeus, and whose sky realm became that of Odin), so she was the subject of much confusion in the Norse mythologies. She was identified as both Odin's daughter and the mother of Frigg. It seems likely that she was an ancient earth goddess whose identity became fused with that of Frigg. Whatever the correct interpretation, both Jorth and Frigg were clearly manifestations of the Goddess in her earth-mother aspect.

As the wife of the supreme deity and mother of his children, Frigg shared many of Hera's characteristics and was venerated as the divine mother of both the Aesir and humanity, who could intercede with her husband on a supplicant's behalf. She was said to live in the palace Fensalir ("sea hall"), where she created clouds by weaving, or solar rays by spinning golden thread. In mythological terms, the most important of her children was the beautiful "good god," Balder ("Lord"). Balder had once dreamed of his premature death, whereupon the frightened Frigg made every living creature promise never to harm her beloved son. However, she deemed the mistletoe too young to be a danger, a fact which the trickster Loki discovered, and, during one of the gods' rowdy games, slipped a dart of mistletoe into the hands of the blind god Höder, who flung it at Balder and killed him. The gods were distraught: Nanna (another earth goddess), Balder's wife, died of grief, and all of nature went into mourning. The myths tell that Balder descended to the underworld realm of the giantess Hel who, after Frigg had entreated her to release her son, agreed to do so if they could find no one who did not lament his death. The crone Thokk (the evil Loki in disguise) refused, and Balder was condemned to remain in the underworld. It was said that he would be resurrected only after the battle of Ragnorak, when he would return to rule the new world.

Below: Freyja in her cat-drawn chariot; Frigg and Freyja are sometimes interchangeable in Germano-Norse myth, for both represent aspects of the Goddess's power over fertility. Background: The bull, sacred to the earth mother Frigg.

The story of Frigg and Balder exhibits clear parallels with that of many other mother goddesses and their son/lovers, including Isis, Osiris and Horus, and also the Virgin Mary and Christ. All symbolically relate to maternal devotion, the undermining of good by evil, the death of nature, but also to eventual redemption. Along with the spindle that she plied, Frigg's primary symbolic attributes — fruits of the earth — were those associated with motherhood and terrestrial fertility. Lesser goddesses of the Norse pantheon also shared Frigg's powers and attributes, including Sif, the golden-haired wife of the thunder god Thor, whose blonde tresses symbolized grain, and Idunn, the guardian of the golden apples that bestowed immortality upon the gods.

Although they are closely linked with the Aesir, the fertility spirits Freyr ("Lord") and his sister, Freyja ("Lady"), belonged to a separate race, the Vani. The siblings had entered the world of the Aesir as hostages following a war between the two supernatural camps. If Frigg was equivalent to the Greco-Roman Hera (Juno), in her aspect as the goddess of love, Freyja most closely corresponds to Aphrodite (Venus), for, according to the Edda, the lovely Freyja was "the most renowned of the goddesses…she enjoys love poetry and it is good to call on her for help in love

affairs." It is more than likely, however, that Frigg and Freyja were artificially separated manifestations of the Goddess, not least because the Old German goddess Frija (from which "Friday," the name of the day that was sacred to her, is derived) is rather confusingly associated with Frigg rather than with Freyja. Many conflicting stories tell of Freyr and Freyja's birth: some say that they were the children of Njord, the god of the waters and ships, others that they were the offspring of mother earth alone. Either way, they were regarded as the guardians of such natural features as lakes and mountains, to which votive offerings were made. Their primary attributes were the golden boar, a fertility symbol, and the ship, an association that may account for the significance of ship burials, for the Vanir were also associated with the spirits of human ancestors who, although buried in the earth or at sea, continued to live on in the Otherworld to which they had sailed.

Her beauty, as well as the fertility that she bestowed, made Freyja the target of the frost giants, who constantly attempted to abduct her, thus inciting the ongoing cosmic conflict that would finally be resolved at Ragnorak. However, the most famous myth relating exclusively to Freyja tells of her desire for the magical necklace called the Brisingamen (which may be associated with the Norse rainbow, Bifröst). So desperate was she to own it that she slept with each of its creators — four dwarves — in turn, thus betraying her husband, Odur, who abandoned her, after which she wandered the earth searching for him and lamenting her loss. Another version of the story tells that Odur was peripatetic by nature, and his frequent absences caused Freyja to shed ruddy tears. The Edda relates that "Freyja has many names, the reason for this being that she called herself now this, now that, when she traveled among strange races looking for

Below: The Germanic earth goddess Hertha clasps a cornucopia representing natural abundance. Her chariot is harnessed to sacred cows, emblems of the maternal principle. Tacitus described her worship under the name of Nerthus, whose veiled image was transported around the countryside. Background: The Norse giantess Hella.

Odur….On her journey she sits in a float driving a pair of cats." The cats that pulled Freyja's chariot were presumably the Norse equivalent of the leonine companions of the Mesopotamian Goddess which, unfortunately, lose much of their symbolic might in this cultural translation. Both Odur and Brisingamen (one of Freyja's most potent symbols) may represent the death of nature, for when Loki stole Brisingamen from Freyja, all vegetation withered, until Heimdall discovered the necklace and restored it to her. Yet Freyja is an ambiguous goddess who held power not only over love and beauty, but also over sorcery and war: therefore, she was far more complex than Aphrodite. One of her many names to which the Edda refers was Syr ("the sow"), and both Freyja and her brother owned boars, named Gullinbursti ("golden bristles") and Hildisvin ("battle pig"), demonstrating their dual aspect as deities of pugnacity as well as fertility, seen also in the belief that Freyja shared the souls of the valiant warriors who had died in battle with Odin.

There are some striking parallels between Germanic and Norse sacred belief that, despite the different names employed, illustrate their common source. In *Germania*, for example, Tacitus attested to the homage paid to the earth mother (Nerthus) that he witnessed among the Germanic tribes, describing how, within a sacred grove on a sea island believed to be the sanctuary of the goddess, priests tended the wagon draped with cloth that she was said to inhabit. At certain times of the year, this shrine made a stately perambulation among the people, bringing the gift of fertility wherever it went. "Whatever place she deigns to honor with her advent and stay… only at that time are peace and quiet known and prized until the goddess…is at last restored…to her temple. After which, the wagon and drape…and the deity herself are bathed in a mysterious pool. The rite is performed by slaves who, as soon as it is done, are drowned in the lake." He also recorded that the Aestii "worship the Mother of the Gods. They wear, as emblem of this cult, the masks of boars. These act as an armor and defense against all things, making the worshippers of the goddess safe even in the midst of their enemies." Both of Tacitus's observations are strikingly similar to the Norse tales relating to Freyja and her attributes.

Although Freyja was a goddess of war, it was the "maidens of Odin," or the Valkyries ("choosers of the slain"), who were more specifically associated with battle, or, more properly, with the glorious afterlife that would be earned by those who had died heroically. Many of their individual names, such as Göll ("screamer") or Hlökk ("shrieker"), reflect the belief that they appeared as crows or ravens on

Above: The early northern Europeans believed that every natural feature was personified by an anima loci ("spirit of the place"). As lesser manifestations of the Goddess, female spirits like these nymphs were associated with water.

the souls of those who had not distinguished themselves by a glorious death in battle were condemned. She was said to be the daughter of Loki, architect of the mass destruction eventually wrought by Ragnarok, and the repulsive giantess Angurboda ("hag of the iron wood"). As an Aesir hybrid, she was given sovereignty by Odin over the world of the dead, Helheim (or Niflheim). Here, it was said, the walls were covered in serpents, and diners ate from a plate called starvation with the help of the knife of hunger, and drank from her cup of darkness. The body of Hel was described as consisting of half-living and half-necrotic flesh: thus her symbolic colors were black and white. Hel and her realm shared many characteristics with the Greek Hecate and Hades, for each was accompanied or guarded by a ferocious hell hound; sometimes Hel rode a black horse—a nightmare—whose appearance heralded death. In the Germanic tradition, Hel was also called Holle (Holla, or Holda). Regarded similarly as the demonic queen of hell, she also had a more benevolent aspect, for she was said to give life to newborns by releasing their souls from her realm. The controller of the weather, she was believed to create snow by shaking her feather-filled cushion, wind, by screaming, and rain by washing her garments.

the battlefield, selecting those who had fought with merit and escorting their souls to Valhalla. There, presided over by Odin, the warriors would enjoy an eternal afterlife tailored to their masculine desires that consisted solely of drinking mead and fighting. Although the Valkyries were sometimes said to transform themselves into swans, mares, or hawks, and—thanks to Richard Wagner's operas—were later romanticized into beautiful young women in horned helmets riding dramatically into battle, they were originally symbolized by scavenging, squabbling crows. This association is underlined by the similar depiction accorded to Celtic war goddesses.

Despite the fact that she was not strictly a goddess, being described in the Edda as a giantess, Hel (or Hella) played a significant role in Norse mythology as ruler of the shadowy realm to which

In the guise of a frog, she retrieved the ripe apple of immortality from her well every year, ensuring that fertility returned to the earth. Furthermore, her annual appearance as a dove brought natural abundance, while the elder tree, which was believed to embody her magical powers of healing, endures as her attribute through its German name *Holunder*.

THE CELTIC GODDESS

Unlike the Norse goddesses, whose stories were immortalized in the Edda, far less information survives regarding their Celtic counterparts, for the Celtic tradition was handed down orally. Only a few mythological cycles—notably those of Ireland and Wales—were preserved in written form. However, it is clear from the recovery of votive offerings and other artefacts, that the Celts regarded the Goddess as associated inextricably with the natural world around them: she thus appears to have been the primary focus of worship. And although each tribe venerated the Goddess under a different name, singling out whichever of her powers was most relevant to their needs, she was common and vital to all versions of Celtic belief. Furthermore, because the number three was regarded as having magical power by the Celts, many of their goddesses were invoked as reinforcing triple entities: virgin, mother and crone, for instance, and many combined the primary qualities of birth, life and death.

To the early Celts, the natural world was the embodiment of the mother goddess.

There was no need to personify her iconically, for her presence was symbolized everywhere aniconically. She existed in the forests (whose groves were designated sacred to her), as well as in the mountains that were regarded as her breasts—a belief reflected in the names of many hills, includ-

Left: The Celts ascribed divinity to features of the landscape around them, believing, for example, that rivers and streams were the sacred preserves of such goddesses as Boann, in Ireland, and Sequana, in Gaul.
Background: *A Celtic shield with a threefold device.*

Left: Although the prehistoric megalith called Stonehenge, in Wiltshire, England, predates the Celtic period, the Celts venerated such standing stones, and particularly holed stones, which were associated with the life-giving and curative powers of the Goddess.

Right and below: The introduction of Christianity into Celtic lands could not entirely suppress the deeply embedded "pagan" view of sanctity. Celtic Christian crosses (right) assumed the form of the solar wheel and were decorated with vegetal and animal motifs, while medieval female figures (below) shared attributes traditionally ascribed to the Goddess. Background: The apple of immortality, sacred to the Celtic Morgans.

ing the Paps of Anu in County Kerry, Ireland. The name Anu is the Munster variation of Danu, the mother of the Irish gods, the Tuatha dé Danaan ("people of the goddess Danu"), who may be equated with Don, her British counterpart. River goddesses, who were associated with fertility, were worshipped extensively by the Celts. Perhaps the most celebrated Irish river goddess was Boann, the spirit of the River Boyne; Sinend represented the Shannon. In Gaul, Axona was goddess of the Aisne, Sequana of the Seine, and the name of the Marne is derived from the Latin *matrona* (divine mother). As illustrated by depictions of Verbeia, the British goddess of the River Wharfe who holds two snakes, these goddesses were frequently symbolized by

serpents, as well as by the duck that Sequana was depicted as riding.

Rivers, lakes, trees and mountains were the foremost natural symbols of the Goddess, but wells were also of great significance. In common with the Norse concept of Yggdrasil, the Celts regarded all aspects of life and death as existing in parallel planes: for example, although the souls of the dead inhabited the Otherworld, they would frequently visit their human descendants in the form of swans wearing silver or gold collars and chains. Indeed, it was through the Goddess that access could be gained to the Otherworld, for by burying their dead, the Celts not only returned them to the womb of mother earth, but also created the passage through which their souls would pass to an eternal paradise where such ninefold goddesses as the Morgans or Korrigens tended the apples of immortality.

However, one did not always need to die to gain access to the Otherworld, or to the

sonifying the afflicted part of the body that the goddess was entreated to heal. And such associations have endured: on the Isle of Skye, a well of fertility is still said to help cattle to calf, while the western European wells now associated with many female Christian saints (who took over the role of the Celtic goddesses that preceded them) still serve as places of prayer, ritually decorated with flowers.

Other man-made Celtic symbols of the Goddess include cairns (which represent the cosmic mountain) and certain standing stones. Although those that assume the form of tall columns are regarded as having masculine, phallic associations, diamond-shaped stones are equated with the feminine principle, their form being reminiscent of the womb. The stones most directly associated with the Goddess are those into which a hole has been bored, and the juxtaposition of "female" and "male" stones can be particularly appreciated at the Men-an-Tol grouping in Cornwall. Such holed stones are still occasionally visited by those who are infertile or sick; they touch the stone, or crawl through the hole, in the hope of a cure. Whether holed or not, many ancient stone formations, such as those at Newgrange in Ireland, were carved by early craftsmen with a spiral decorative motif; this symbol also represents the Goddess, for its serpentine shape recalls the snake and water, as well as the perpetually dynamic motion of life.

Through the written myths that have survived, it is clear that the help of goddesses of the land had to be enlisted if the human tribe was to sur-

Left: Van Gogh's evocative painting of wheat sheaves, associated with most Celtic fertility goddesses, and especially with the Romano-Celtic matronae: *wheat was a staple food that sprang up from the body of mother earth.* **Below:** *One of the most sacred Druid fertility rites involved cutting the mistletoe (a Goddess symbol because of its moonlike berries) from the sacred "masculine" oak tree. The golden sickle used to harvest the mistletoe recalls the crescent moon.* **Background:** *Celtic knotwork symbolizing the cycles of time: birth, life and death.*

Goddess's fecund womb, for it could be reached by means of the man-made well (like the apple, a symbol of the Morgans) or by a shaft sunk into the earth. It was said that the source of the Boyne, for example, was Conla's Well, its water, which originated in the Otherworld, bestowing wisdom on all who drank it. Boann challenged its power by walking round it three times, but three waves surged from the well and drowned her, whereupon she became the spirit of the river. There were many well goddesses, including Coventina (originally a Celtic goddess who was later renamed by the Romans), to whom a well on Hadrian's Wall was sacred; like all her counterparts, she was said to be able to restore fertility to barren women and to heal the sick. Archaeologists have recovered many votive offerings that were flung into wells. Some were objects of value, including coins, but others were clay objects fashioned in the shape of a human limb—often a hand—presumably per-

Above: Rackham's depiction of the magician Merlin's enchantment by Nimuë. Celtic legends abound with such witchlike figures, who are aspects of the Goddess as crone. Background: A Celtic emblem that combines the triads of feminity and masculinity to form a fourfold symbol of the guardian goddess Eriu, an earth mother.

treated cruelly by her husband, and her brother, Bran, rode to her rescue only to be killed, causing Branwen to die of grief. The tale is mirrored by that of Finonnula and her brothers, the Irish children of Lir, who were transformed into swans before being mercifully released by death. The message implicit in these mythological stories also has a Christian implication: wrongs inflicted (on the land) must be endured until avenged by a future hero. Yet some mythological heroines were not so passive: Macha, for instance, defeated her rival male claimants to the rulership of Ulster in battle. The belief that ownership of the land lay with the Goddess is also illustrated in the tale of the invasion of Ireland by the Milesians, who promised each of the island's three guardian goddesses — Banba, Fodla and Eriu — that her name would be given to the country. It was Eriu who handed the Milesians a ritual cup to confirm her acceptance, and, indeed, Ireland's present name, Eire, is derived from hers.

The Celts were a warlike people, and their mythology constantly underlines this preoccupation, not least in the form of their war goddesses, of whom the Irish Morrigan was probably the most terrible. The Morrigan was regarded as both a single and a triple entity; in the latter instance, the Morrigan ("specter") was joined by her sisters Babd ("rage"), and Nemain ("frenzy"), whose horrible howl caused a hundred warriors to die of fright. Like the Germano-Norse Valkyries, they were said to haunt the battlefield in the form of crows, their very appearance causing sufficient panic to rout an army; they also had the gift of prophecy, and were said to wash the weapons of those who were about to die in battle in a nearby ford.

Celtic mythology reveals a very highly developed concept of the Goddess in her hag or crone aspect. The Irish Cailleach, or "veiled one," incorporates the Goddess's creator aspect, for she is associated with

vive and triumph. Thus, for example, the supreme Irish god, the Dagda ("father of all"), mated with Boann (as well as with the war goddess, the Morrigan), symbolically allying the *anima loci* with the human tribe. Queen Medb (who derived her superhuman strength from bathing in a magical well each day) also granted territorial sovereignty to nine successive Irish kings of Connacht through sexual union. Sometimes the goddess who conferred such sovereignty had to be sacrificed, as seen in the sad story of the Welsh heroine Branwen, the daughter of Llyr, god of the sea, who was married to Matholwch, king of Ireland. She was mis-

the making of mountains, yet is also the guardian of the cauldron of wisdom and plenty, thus combining the Goddess's unfathomable knowledge with the gift of fertility that she may bestow upon the worthy. The primary attribute of the crone Goddess is her cauldron, which is both a symbol of abundance as the communal cooking vessel and, like the well, a source of wisdom. Thus, for example, the Irish Niall of the Nine Hostages becomes king of Tara because he alone is willing to embrace the foul hag who guards the sacred well. Welsh myth tells of the cauldron of the crone Kerridwen (alternatively called "the old sow" for her fertility function), from which she sometimes fed favored recipients (including her son Afagddu, whose hideousness she tried to mitigate). It was said that as the boy Gwion, the bard Taliesin was accidentally splashed by the contents of the cauldron, whereupon he gained all knowledge. The furious Kerridwen pursued him, changing herself successively into a greyhound (symbolizing her mastery over the earth), an otter (the water), a songbird and a falcon (air), and finally, a red hen (fire), whereupon she gobbled up Gwion, who had transformed himself into a grain of corn. He was later reborn from her body,

whereupon she placed him in a leather bag and cast him into the water, from which he was eventually rescued. Yet despite her generally aged aspect, the Cailleach was an ambivalent figure, for she could transform herself into a beautiful girl, illustrating symbolically the transition of the seasons of winter (Samhain) into spring (Imbolg).

Although, unlike the Norse tales, the Celtic mythologies do not tell of a goddess of love, there are many goddesses of wisdom, notably the Irish Brigit ("high one"), daughter of the Dagda. It was she to whom the annual festival of Imbolg was dedicated on February 1, for she was the guardian of

Above: The Celts dedicated groves of trees to the Goddess as her sacred sites.
Below, left: After Christianity suppressed Celtic sacred beliefs, the crone's cauldron of abundance became an instrument of witchcraft. *Below: The medieval "goddess" retained her mastery over animals, as seen in this French tapestry.* *Background: The beehive of Nantosuelta, goddess of the home.*

Right: *Numerous Christian saints, including the martyr St. Cecilia (portrayed here by Raphael in 1513), are believed to be legendary rather than historical figures. Cecilia was tortured horribly for refusing to worship the gods of Rome. Here she holds the organlike instrument she played to drown out the sound of pagan music. Many ancient goddesses—especially in Mesopotamia— had musical instruments as attributes.*

such domestic creatures as cattle and sheep, patroness of childbirth, and bestower of fertility on all vegetation. Like Athena/Minerva, her domains included those of learning, poetry (the verbal form in which tribal lore was communicated),

agriculture and smithcraft. Her worshippers sometimes regarded her as three separate entities: the Brigits of wisdom, healing and the blacksmith's craft. Symbolized by such animals as cows, and by grain, Brigit's other attributes include the well of healing or wisdom, and the rowan tree, which was thought to possess curative properties. After the coming of Christianity to Ireland, Brigit was translated into St. Brigid (or St. Bride) of Kildare—also the patron of poets, blacksmiths and healers, who was symbolized by the cow that magically produced milk three times a day. Unsurprisingly, the saint's feast day falls on February 1, and the various ways in which St. Bride's Day is traditionally celebrated also attest to her pagan origins: a corn dolly being carried from house to house, for example, or an oat dolly being placed in a straw cradle with a wooden wand.

Reflecting the close association of Celtic goddesses with the natural world, animals were often regarded as their symbols. As we have seen, ravens or crows represented death; serpents, fertility; while swans were believed to be spirits from the Otherworld. The Iceni Andraste, "invincible one," who was associated with the Saxon Eostra—the moon goddess who was said to lay (Easter) eggs—was symbolized by the hare that Boudicca released ritually before battle, making it a symbol of victory as well as fertility. Many Irish goddesses, including the Morrigan, owned magical cows, but the Gaulish Damona was actually represented as a cow, crowned with corn and attended by serpents. As in many other cultures, the bear was regarded as a fiercely maternal creature: thus Arduinna, the goddess of the Ardennes Forest, was represented as a bear (although she was also depicted riding a boar), as was Artio. Other Celtic goddesses, particularly those associated with healing, were represented in the company of dogs, which, because they howl at the moon, were believed to be able to harness its curative powers. One of the most popular Gaulish goddesses was Epona, the horse goddess depicted with a mare's head, who represented the fertility of domestic animals.

Just as the Celtic goddess of sovereignty had been used to sanction the rulership of a male god or tribe (a universal pattern), Roman invaders of Celtic lands legitimized indigenous fertility goddesses as objects of worship by making them the consorts of Roman gods. The Gaulish Rosmerta, goddess of prosperity (symbolized, like Fortuna, by the rudder-surmounted globe, and by the money bag, bucket, ladle and cornucopia) became the "wife" of Mercury. Nantosuelta, the Gaulish goddess of the home depicted both with a scepter surmounted by a house and with a beehive, was made the consort of Sucellus. Yet although Romanized, the significance of the Celtic goddess survived, as can be seen in the numerous *matronae* (divine mothers) representations of this period, in which three seated women are shown surrounded by symbolic attributes of fertility: cornucopiae, children, bread, grain, fruit, spindles, and also dogs and trees. Indeed, although they tried, neither the Romans nor the Christians could eradicate the Goddess's deeply entrenched position in the sacred beliefs of western Europe.

Below: Raphael's portrait of St. Catherine, whose existence is now a subject of doubt. The ritual adornment of her image by young girls on her feast day, November 25, unwittingly emulates rites connected to the worship of the ancient Goddess.
Background: *Entwined seahorses, an emblem of Epona.*

The Indian Subcontinent and Far East

In a cursory examination, it would appear that, dominated as they are by male entities, the major religions of the Indian Subcontinent and Far East accord little significance to their goddesses, designating them only a supporting role as their male counterparts' loyal consorts. In Hinduism, for example, Brahma, Vishnu and Shiva comprise the compact *trimurti* (trinity) that regulates the cosmos. Thus it would seem that each has respectively usurped one of the triple functions of the Goddess as creator, preserver and destroyer, thereby excluding her from any meaningful power. But this assumption is, in fact, far from the truth. For although specific Hindu cults, such as Tantric Hinduism, have a highly developed concept of the importance of the Goddess, most Hindus also believe that the god is powerless without his *shakti*—the feminine principle that is both embodied in the god and represented by his goddess "wife." Furthermore, innumerable Goddess cults remain vibrant among Hindus. Although Buddhism does not recognize even the Buddha as a supernatural deity, considering him instead the wisest of mortal teachers, the few female figures traditionally associated with Buddhism in India, such as Siddhartha Gautama's mother, Maya, are accorded the unmistakable attributes of the Goddess. Yet following the spread of Buddhism to Tibet, China and Japan, the indigenous goddesses of these countries were integrated into the emergent system of sacred belief as bodhisattvas—much as many Celtic goddesses survived in the guise of Christian saints. Moreover, some ancient goddesses were just too powerful to be obliterated: the worship of Amaterasu, for example, not only endured in Japan, but the goddess was venerated as the supreme being. The active worship of the Goddess, in whatever form, testifies to her resonance in these regions, even in modern times.

THE HINDU GODDESS

When the Aryan initiators of Hinduism invaded India between 1500 and 1000 BC, they encountered a major fertility cult focused upon the regenerative powers of the Goddess (*devi*). Although the characteristics of the cult varied according to whichever aspect of nature was most important to a locality—agriculture or animal husbandry, for example—it was the Goddess, not a god, who was considered the supreme regulator of fertility. Although the Aryans later imposed their own sacred beliefs upon the Indus Valley and the Ganges Plain, the veneration of the mother goddess (*mahadevi*) specific to a particular locality remained paramount to her worshippers and continues to this day. Indeed, most

Opposite: Sengen-Sama, goddess of Mount Fujiyama. She holds the sacred sakaki twig and touches the magical jewel around her neck.
Below: The fanged Hindu goddess Hayagriva emerges from a shell (a yoni symbol). Background: A Hindu shakti.

57

villages still venerate the Goddess in the form of an ancient painted stone, but more elaborate representations, like those that depict the early vegetal goddesses (*vrikshadevatas*) kicking trees as a stimulus to the burgeoning of life, remain common. The festivals celebrating such deities as Manasa, who is believed to protect against venomous snake bites in Bengal, Bihar, Orissa and Assam, have similarly ancient origins. Indeed, such is her resonance that even among ordinary modern Hindus, the cult of the Goddess (for she is still worshipped generically, as well as in her individual aspects) rivals those of Vishnu and Shiva, the two more active members of the *trimurti.*

Despite this age-old veneration of the Goddess, truly orthodox Hinduism recognizes a masculine-dominated pantheon, which evolved from the thirty-three Vedic deities of the sky, atmosphere and earth that are described in the Vedas (c. 1200–500 BC). However, even though such male deities as Prajapati and Brahma were later cast in the role of creators, this honor really belongs to the Goddess in the form of Aditi, the primordial sacred cow from whose milk the universe was churned into existence, and who was regarded as the mother of the gods. Moreover, Aditi was linked with Prithivi, the cosmic cow, who was the wife of the supreme Vedic god, Dyaus, and who nourished all from her teats. Even today, as the representatives of the mother goddess, Hindus treat cows with extreme respect, regarding their body products—even dung—as sacred purifying substances. After their birth, such gods as Indra, Varuna and Rudra appear to have taken over primary control of the universe, but the Goddess was not entirely excluded. Of great importance among the Vedic goddesses, for example, was Ushas, the goddess of the dawn, personified as a rose-clad woman whose chariot was drawn across the sky by russet-colored cows, and who, some said, was simultaneously the daughter and consort of the creator god Prajapati, and thus the mother of all living creatures. Vac, the wife of Indra, also represented as a cow, was venerated as the goddess who gave speech, mantras and the Sanskrit alphabet to humans. She was said to have first pronounced the sacred sound "Om" (called the *mantramatika,* "mother of the mantras", or "sound of creation") and who, in some traditions, created the Vedic gods by speaking their names aloud.

From the Vedic deities evolved the Hindu pantheon, with the male *trimurti* at its head, apparently incorporating the vital functions of the cosmos: creation (Brahma), preservation (Vishnu) and destruction (Shiva). However, the Goddess, as Bhavani ("giver of existence"), is said to have given birth to the divine triad. Indeed, so profound was the grip that she held on her worshippers that not only were the many local *matres* preserved by "marriage" to the Hindu gods, but many Hindu temples are still dedicated pre-eminently to her. Furthermore, as illustrated in the myth of the creation of Durga, it becomes clear that without their *shaktis* —feminine sides— male gods are powerless. Faced with the disastrous threat of a buffalo demon that only a feminine deity could destroy, the psychic waves of fury that emanated from each god merged and consolidated in the form of Durga. Her head was formed from Shiva's enraged energy, her waist from Indra's, her eyes from Agni's, her arms from Vishnu's and her feet from Brahma's. Other versions of the myth say that the gods called upon the Goddess, who manifested herself independently of their aid. Both versions agree, however, that once incarnated, this beautiful goddess, mounted on her mighty lion, first seduced the demon and then beheaded him.

The Goddess as *shakti* has special significance in the beliefs and rituals of Tantric Hinduism (as well as of Tantric Buddhism), which derive from the texts of the Tantras. These practitioners seek to develop the spiritual power (*siddhi*) inherent in each individual in order to attain liberation (*jivanmukti*). Because they believe that the human body is a microcosm of the universe, the primary cosmic forces—that of Shiva, regarded as being the passive, masculine principle, and that of the *shakti*, the active, feminine principle— identified as existing in dynamic opposition, are also present in every person. Thus the primary Tantric form of yoga—kundalini—is devoted to awakening the *shakti*, believed to reside at the base of the spine, and raising it upward through the seven wheels (*chakras*) of spiritual energy located at successive points in the spine, until the *shakti* reaches the head, where the Goddess unites with Shiva, bringing bliss and enlightenment to the practitioner. While the *chakras* are symbolized by wheels or lotus blooms, the *shakti* is envisaged as a fiery coiled serpent, which, as it ascends, unwinds slowly and sinuously. Tantric worshippers of the *shakti* are collectively termed *Shaktas*; they not only practice kundalini yoga, but may also recite the mantras specific to the *shakti*, or they

Left: *Hindu depictions of mother goddesses emphasize their powers of fertility through voluptuous bodies, benevolent expressions and ornamental symbols of abundance.*

Background: *Rajasthan image of a sphinx-like winged tiger.*

Above: *Shiva the destroyer in the form of Nataraja, lord of the dance of creation and destruction. The ring of fire can be equated with a yoni symbol, illustrating the power of the female* shakti *that energizes Shiva's masculine potency.*

Background: *Brahma and his consort Sarasvati.*

may meditate on a mandala or yantra that brings them spiritually closer to the Goddess. Such meditational aids include the *sri yantra*, in which the *shakti* is represented by downward-pointing triangles, colored in the Goddess's traditional hues of black (*tamas*), red (*rajas*) and white (*sattva*); in this context, the Goddess may be known as Prakriti. Another important symbol of the female principle is the *yoni* circle, which, like the triangle, is an aniconic depiction of female genitalia, often seen in conjunction with Shiva's *lingam*, a phallic symbol (in fact, the circle within which Shiva, as Nataraja, is depicted as dancing has been described as a *yoni*).

Thus Tantric Hinduism is focused upon the Goddess as *shakti*, venerating her as the force of creativity that animates the cosmos. In this aspect, she is celebrated for her uninhibited sexuality. Tantric Buddhism, too, may represent such goddesses as Nairatmya, the deity of liberty, or Visvamata ("all mother"), entwined in an ecstatic

embrace with their male partners (in these instances, the buddhas Hevjara and Kalacakra). As in many other cultures, the Goddess may also take the forms of virgin (such as Kumari, an aspect of Parvati) or crone (like Kubjika, the goddess of potters). However, for ordinary Hindus, the Goddess is more usually worshipped either as one of the numerous local mother goddesses, or as one of the consorts of the *trimurti*. The former category includes, for example, the Bengali Shashti ("the sixth"), deity of childbirth, who rides a cat and receives thanks on the sixth day after the birth of a child, and the red-garbed smallpox goddess, Sitala (euphemistically called "the cool one" to placate her), who travels the country on an ass demanding worship.

Just as Brahma is regarded as a somewhat abstract deity who receives little active worship, his wife Sarasvati ("flowing one") arouses less passion among her worshippers than do the wives of Vishnu or Shiva. She was originally a water goddess, the spirit of the River Sarasvati, as indicated when a crescent moon is pictured on her brow. Later, she took on the characteristics of Vac, in that she was believed to be the originator of the Sanskrit language. Today she is regarded as the goddess of learning and all artistic pursuits. Although she may be shown seated on the lotus (not only a *yoni* symbol, but the emblem of perfection and fertility depicted with most benign Hindu goddesses) she is more often represented holding manuscripts or musical instruments, with a peacock as her mount. Its eyelike feathers symbolize the celestial stars, which she shares with Brahma.

The peacock is also the vehicle of Lakshmi, Vishnu's beautiful, gentle and devoted wife, the goddess of good fortune and wealth. It was said that she was created from Aditi's primordial ocean of milk as a result of the gods' quest for *soma* (the elixir of immortality). Using the cosmic mountain, Mandara, as a pole, and Vasuki, the serpent, as a rope, they churned the milk to no avail, until Vishnu transformed himself into the tortoise Kurma and completed the task. Lakshmi (also known as Ksirabdhitanaya, "daughter of the ocean of milk," and Jaladhija, "ocean born") was the fortunate by-product. She became Vishnu's beloved consort and accompanied him during each of his subsequent incarnations (*avatars*). She appeared as a lotus when he came to earth as Vamama the dwarf; as Sita ("the furrow"), the wife of Rama, who was kidnapped by the demon king Ravana; and as Radha ("she elephant"), Krishna's favorite *gopi* (milkmaid). In all of these appearances, she demonstrated her loyalty and selfless love for Vishnu. As the lotus goddess—an aspect of Matripadma, the golden lotus mother from which some believe the cosmos emerged—Lakshmi is called Kamala or Padma, who was born as a lotus from Vishnu's forehead, and is represented as standing on, or holding, a lotus. As Sita, she may be symbolized by a basket filled with rice, representing agricultural abundance and confirming her association with Sri ("prosperity"). Divali, the "festival of lights" held at the beginning of winter, is devoted to Lakshmi. During its course, oil lamps are lit to guide the goddess into mortal homes, and motifs (*rangoli*) of lotuses are drawn on the floor to welcome her, in the hope that she will bless the household with good luck and prosperity.

While Lakshmi is represented as the ideal spouse who is lovely, benevolent, and true, Shiva's consorts—Sati, Parvati, Durga, Kali and Ganga—collectively represent much more varied qualities (although the first pair share many of Lakshmi's characteristics). It is said that Sati's father, Daksha, did not invite her husband to a sacrifice, a snub that caused Sati such shame that she committed suicide by burning herself alive (the origination of the now outlawed practice of *suttee*). In his grief, Shiva

danced wildly with her corpse (or presumably with what remained of it) until Vishnu, fearful that the earth would be destroyed, dismembered her body. Pilgrimages (*pitha*) are still made to the places where pieces of Sati's body are believed to have fallen, and Tantric Hindus believe that the shrine in Assam where her *yoni* fell, is the most sacred. Sati was subsequently reincarnated in Parvati, the daughter of the Himalayas, whose sacred mountain is Annapurna. Many tales tell

Below: This stone carving at Bharhut, of Chulakoka Devata, dates from the first century BC. The goddess stimulates the growth of her sacred tree by kicking its roots. The wheels on the left represent chakras, centers of spiritual energy.
Background: The serpent, associated with Lakshmi.

Above: *The peacock serves as mount to several Hindu goddesses, including Sarasvati and Lakshmi, and to Brahma and Parvati's son, Skanda, as well. Its magnificent plumage evokes both the beauty of the Goddess and her all-encompassing vision, represented by its many feathered "eyes."*

Background: *The devouring crocodile.*

of Parvati's love for Shiva: one says that he rejected her initial approaches on account of her dark color, which contrasted unfavorably with his skin, whitened by the ashes traditionally daubed on the bodies of ascetics, whereupon she practiced asceticism (*tapas*) so rigorously that her body glowed. Shiva was now attracted to her, but decided to test her loyalty by transforming himself into a dwarf and, in this form, vilifying himself. Parvati defended him and was rewarded with marriage to the god. Another version goes further, saying that Parvati shed her dark skin like a snake, thereby revealing the golden skin that shone underneath (in which form she is known as Gauri—"golden one"). Parvati became the mother of Ganesha and

Skanda by Shiva, and lived relatively happily within this family unit, although she was often plagued by her jealousy of another of Shiva's wives, Ganga. She is worshipped as a mother goddess, and her symbols are those of abundance and nourishment: a ladle, and bowls of rice and milk. At the fall festival of Annakuta ("mountain of food") in Varanasi, she is presented with offerings of food, which are then distributed among the poor.

The link between the benevolent Parvati and the terrible Kali is explained in mythology: the dark sheath of skin that Parvati sloughed off became Kali, "the black one." Indeed, in Tantric representations, Kali may be shown dancing on the supine body of Shiva, who lies in a close embrace with Parvati. Thus his two wives are collaborating, Parvati enticing him into the world, and Kali spurring him into procreative action. Kali is the ultimate terrible mother—creator and destroyer—who, having killed the demon Raktavijra, drank his blood to prevent its falling to the ground and creating thousands more demons. She is now believed to be sustained by blood, which is depicted dripping from her withered tongue, and which her devotees must offer her (the decoration of their hands with henna is a related tradition). Representations of Kali may show her in the cemetery grounds she is believed to inhabit, wearing a necklace of skulls and a serpent as a collar (representing *kundalini* energy), as well as a belt of severed hands; her forehead is adorned with the third eye and crescent moon of Shiva. She may wield a sword or hold a severed head in her hand. Her symbols include the black pot and the mirror of the abyss. Although unequivocally associated with the symbols of death, Kali, through such attributes as blood and the pot of abundance, is also a goddess of life, who will treat her worshippers kindly.

The destructive Kali is also closely associated with Durga ("the unapproachable one"), who killed the buffalo demon. This is the most famous legend associated with Durga, and her primary symbols relate to this battle. They include the lion upon which she rode and which devoured the demon's lifeless body; the trident of Shiva, or scimitar or spear of the fire god Agni, and the discus of Vishnu. In this Amazonian form, she is also known as Candi ("wrathful"), the goddess additionally associated with the moon and a protector against wild animals, or as Chamunda. Although Durga, as a war goddess, may seem more akin to the bloodthirsty Kali, she is also equated with the benevolent Parvati, as is seen in the story celebrated each year in Bengal during the fall festival of Durgapuja. Like Parvati, Durga is jealous of her husband's other wife, Ganga, the goddess of the River Ganges, and once a year seeks refuge in her parental home in Calcutta. At the end of the festival, however, she must float bitterly along the Ganges itself to its source, the Himalayas, to return to her husband.

Kali and Durga, or Durga and Parvati, are to some extent interchangeable, but what of the rival goddess who causes them so much pain? According to the Puranas, Ganga was once the goddess of the Milky Way who, impressed by the asceticism of the sage Bhagiratha, agreed to descend to earth to purify the ashes of the 60,000 sons of King Sagara. She asked Shiva to break her fall, and he caught her in his matted locks, from which the Ganges is now said to flow gently, bestowing life-giving water on the people of India. Thus depictions of Ganga are usually inseparable from those of Shiva, in whose hair she nestles, clasping a bowl and a lotus—both symbols of watery abundance. She is sometimes represented riding a crocodile, or the mythical makara (half fish, half crocodile), or in the hybrid form of a mermaid. The Ganges personified by the goddess is the most sacred river in Hinduism: those who bathe in it, especially

Left: Despite her decline in many other cultures, the Hindu Goddess in her manifold aspects of creator, preserver and destroyer still commands devoted worship among her followers. This image evokes her procreative and nurturing powers.

Background: *Kali dancing on the body of Shiva.*

at the city of Banaras, will receive its gift of purification. Another important site is the confluence of the Ganges, the Sarasvati and the Yamuna, sacred to the compassionate goddess Yami, sister of Yama, god of the dead, who caused the river to be created. Annual pilgrimages are made here.

Perhaps nowhere else in the world—at least in modern times—is the Goddess in all her multifaceted, often conflicting, aspects, so venerated as in India. And although her active worship is mainly a feature of Hinduism, she has a place in the sacred traditions that are not usually associated with the worship of deities. In Jainism, for example, in which Hindu deities are revered (although not believed to have yet attained the desired state of liberation), the images of such goddesses as Lakshmi and the mother goddess Ambika, who are said to have helped the tirthankaras ("builders of the ford"), stand outside Jain temples. Furthermore, both of Mahavira's mothers (his "conception" and his "birth" mother) dreamed of the goddess Sri (one of fourteen auspicious symbols) before his birth.

TIBETAN, CHINESE AND JAPANESE GODDESSES

Although it originated in India, in terms of the number of its adherents, Buddhism is no longer a significant faith in that country. However, in the lands to which it spread—especially Tibet, China and Japan—it remains a dominant system of sacred belief. Just as Buddha eschewed the exclusive worship of deities in favor of "the third way," so Buddhists recognize the Hindu deities, but do not rely upon them for the attainment of enlightenment and release from the eternal cycle of reincarna-

Background: The cherry, sacred to Maya.

Right: Shichi Gutei Butsomo, the mother of all Buddhas (who can be equated with Prajnaparamita or the maternal White Tara), is the embodiment of perfect wisdom, who gives birth to, nurtures and imparts her knowledge to future Buddhas. In Tantric Buddhism this deity, clearly derived from the Goddess in her maternal aspect, is regarded as Buddha's shakti.

tion. While Buddha himself is unequivocally identified as the mortal Siddhartha Gautama, the name of his mother, Maya, is also that of the Hindu and Buddhist goddess of illusion, as well as of the giver of life. Furthermore, in common with the Christian Virgin Mary, Maya experienced a form of virgin birth: after dreaming that a white elephant had entered her side, she discovered her pregnancy. She gave birth to Buddha from her right side while supported by the tree that is now sacred to her—variously described as a cherry, hawthorn or may—and died of bliss seven days later (so that the womb that bore him would not be sullied by another child). On her death, she joined the ranks of the goddesses.

To the extent that Buddhists of the Indian subcontinent do acknowledge goddesses, it is the Hindu goddesses who are venerated for the assistance that they give to Buddha and, moreover, to all good people. However, within the Buddhist traditions of Tibet, China and Japan, most goddesses are those that were already worshipped in these countries, who were merged with a specific Buddhist bodhisattva—a future Buddha who has already attained enlightenment, but has chosen to delay his or her departure to a higher plane in order to assist humans. The most important such female figure within Tibetan Buddhism is Tara (sGrol-ma), the savioress, who has twenty-one aspects. As the maternal White Tara, for example, sGrol-ma is equated with Prajnaparamita, the mother of the bodhisattvas, who educates her fledglings in supreme wisdom, yet who is also said to have been formed from a tear shed by the bodhisattva Avalokiteshvara, the compassionate one. As the maternal Green Tara (or Bribsun), she accompanies and aids Avalokiteshvara. (It is popularly believed that King Srong-btsan-sgam-po (d. c. AD 650) had both Chinese and Nepalese wives, who were reincarnations of the White and

Green Taras respectively. They helped establish Buddhism in Tibet. In many of her incarnations, Tara may be represented with the omniscient third eye in her forehead, and with other eyes set within the palms of her hands. Kurukulle is the Red Tara, the patroness of love and wealth, who may be depicted bearing weapons, or symbols of divine charity. Another important Tibetan Buddhist goddess is Sridevi, the guardian of the Dalai Lama and also the maintainer of justice who records human transgressions; she shares this judicial role with the indigenous Tibetan goddess, Sipe Gyalmo, who rides a red mule and is represented with three eyes and six arms that grasp a victory flag, a sword, a skull-bowl and a trident (all martial symbols), but also the parasol of sovereignty and the swastika that brings good fortune.

Sipe Gyalmo belongs to the early Tibetan Bon tradition that was largely integrated into Buddhism; however, elements of Bon remain, as in the myth that tells of the creation of the cosmos from the body parts of a female serpent. Similarly, although Buddhism swept through China and Japan, aspects of their more ancient traditions of sacred belief survived—either in separate form, or merged with Buddhist mythology—with the result that many goddesses of different origins appear to coexist quite happily. Wu, a form of shamanism, is believed to have been the earliest form of Chinese sacred belief, but in 213 BC, during the progressive Han dynasty, all books were burned, making it difficult to unravel the many interconnected mythological strands and trace them back to their sources. Thus it is difficult to date the emergence of Nu Kua (also known as Nü Wa, the "snail maiden"), the serpent-tailed goddess who created humans by molding members of the nobility from yellow clay, and ordinary people from drops of muddy water. Despite her uncertain origins, however, she is still venerated today as the

Left: A Buddhist bodhisattva surrounded by sacred symbols of her role as a helper of humans. Many indigenous goddesses remain objects of veneration in those lands that adopted Buddhism, including Tibet, China and Japan, through their transformation into bodhisattvas.

Background: The parasol of nobility.

patroness of marriage. The religious philosophies that subsequently came to hold sway in China were Confucianism (whose principles encouraged the veneration of ancestors and filial piety), Taoism and, of course, Buddhism.

Taoism is focused on the conflicting principles of *yin* (the black, negative and passive feminine principle associated with coldness, wetness, darkness and the moon) and *yang* (the white, positive and active male principle equated with warmth, dryness, light and the sun) that are believed to regulate the universe. If they are in harmony, a state of perfection has been achieved. This concept is best illustrated in the *yin-yang* symbol, in which the opposing principles are equally balanced within a circle of unity; each contains a circle of the other's color within its sigmoid half, thus symbolizing the seed of each that is contained within its opposite. In the *I Ching* divination system, the forces of *yin* and *yang* are represented within the *pa kua* trigrams

*Below: This dynamic
Tantric Buddhist depiction
of the union of Visvamata
("all mother") and
Kalacakra vividly
celebrates the* shakti *power
of the Goddess.*
Background: *The White
Dragon Mother,
Ch'ing Dynasty.*

and *koua* hexagrams as broken lines (*yin*) and continuous lines (*yang*). Although neither principle is regarded as superior to the other, it is interesting that the qualities associated with *yang* are those of the Goddess the world over. Within mythology, many creatures are accorded either *yin* or *yang* characteristics, with *yin* creatures generally traditional to the Goddess—the hen, or the serpent, for example. Furthermore, during the mid-fall festival held on the fifteenth day of the eighth moon (the fall equinox, when the moon is at its fullest), women bake moon cakes and offer them at sacred altars—clearly an age-old form of Goddess worship that has somehow survived to this day.

The venerable Chinese goddess of the moon is Ch'ang O, daughter of Ho Po, lord of the Yellow River (Yangtse) and wife of the archer Yi, who inhabits the sun palace. Ch'ang O, however, lives in the freezing palace of the moon to which she was banished: some myths say that she gained immortality by stealing a pill made from the peaches of immortality that Hsi Wang Mu had given Yi; others, that she drank the elixir of immortality made by the hare in the moon. Both versions agree that she now takes the form of a three-legged toad (each leg symbolizing a ten-day phase of the moon). Another celestial deity is Chih Nü, the "weaving maiden" (the star Vega), whose love affair with Ch'ien Niu, the "ox boy" (the star Altair) caused both to neglect their duties. This enraged the queen of heaven, who separated them with her hairpin, creating the celestial rent that became the River Han (Milky Way). Once a year, however, on the seventh day of the seventh moon, magpies (symbols of joy) build a bridge so that the lovers can be reunited. As Tanabata and Shokujo, the couple is celebrated on July 7 in Japan.

The most important indigenous Chinese goddess is Hsi Wang Mu, the queen mother of the west. She is said to live in a golden, jewel-encrusted palace in the Hsi T'ien western paradise situated in the K'un Lun mountain, an *axis mundi* that has been identified with the Hindu Kush. Around the base of the mountain flow the Black, White, Red and Blue Rivers, but the fifth, the Yellow River, flows from this source through China. Meadows of coriander, grain and sesame grow abundantly on the mountain's slopes, and precious gems like pearls (lunar attributes) and jade (a symbol of the immortality that it is believed to bestow in its liquid form) blossom on the trees that grow around the Lake of Jewels. But the most important fruits in Hsi Wang Mu's heavenly garden are the peaches that take 3,000 years to grow and 3,000 more to ripen. They are finally ready to consume on her birthday, when she invites the other deities to a great banquet, culminating in the serving of the peaches, which confer immortality. Although they are Hsi Wang Mu's most important symbol, she may also be depicted astride a white crane, attended by flocks of bluebirds, or in a chariot drawn by dragons. Her other attendants are three red-headed birds, or the five Yü Nü (the "jade maidens," representing the four cardinal directions and the center), who cool her with their fans. Her mother-goddess association is confirmed by the fact that her element is metal, which is associated with the west and with fall, and provides the material for harvesting tools. Although some myths say that she was the consort of Tung Wang Kung, king of the east, it is more likely that Hsi Wang Mu was an ancient, benevolent mother goddess who possessed the gift of life; indeed, today she is especially venerated by women on their fiftieth birthdays. The only female among the Eight Taoist Immortals is Ho Hsien-ku, who shares the peach as an attribute, as well the lotus, which she may ride on her adventures.

Other significant Chinese goddesses are celebrated in the Taoist tradition. Tao Mu ("the mother of the Tao"), for example—also known as Chun T'i, T'ien Hou, T'ien Mu or Tou Mu—is worshipped as the mother of the celestial ladle (the seven constellations that make up the Great Bear). Her chariot is pulled by seven pigs.

She was described as the mother, by Tou Fu, of nine sons (whose names signified celestial bravery, official, pillar, heart, creature, support, minor, bud and sail) who became the first human kings, while she continued to live in her palace in the Pole Star. This goddess is also venerated by Hindus (as Maritchi) and by Tantric Buddhists, in whose depictions her eight arms may hold the sun, moon, sword, spear, bow, ax, flag, lotus, or wheel. Like many Celtic goddesses, she may be represented with three faces, one of which is that of a sow, explained by the tradition that a Tibetan abbess believed to be a reincarnation of the goddess had a tumor on her neck shaped like a sow's ear. However, her most profound symbol

Above: The base of this throne is decorated with lotus flowers, representing enlightenment and perfection, while the figure's hand gestures, or mudras, have highly specific symbolic meanings. Left: The yin-yang circle illustrates the opposition and potential reconciliation of the female yin (represented in black) and the masculine yang (white) forces that Taoists believe exist within every aspect of the universe.

Right: In China, the crane is regarded as a yin creature, and, since it was believed to live for centuries, symbolizes long life. The white crane is the mount of the queen mother of the west, Hsi Wang Mu, whose peaches also represent immortality.

Below: The Far Eastern bodhisattva of compassion—Kwan-Yin in China, Kannon in Japan—surrounded by lotus blossoms and wearing in her headdress the image of Amitabha, the "impersonal Buddha," who preached that enlightenment can be achieved by faith.

remains the seven stars of the Great Bear that adorn the flags of Taoist monasteries. Ma Ku ("the hemp lady") had three incarnations: as the planter of mulberry trees; as the compassionate daughter of a cruel father; and as a hermit. Her image is presented to those who have achieved their silver and golden wedding anniversaries. The three K'eng San Hu-niang ("lavatory ladies") are guardians of the "golden bushel of troubled origins," often represented in the form of a red bucket that was, until recently, a traditional wedding present. It symbolized not only everyday natural bodily functions but also childbirth, of which they are the supervising deities.

Another female figure associated with the birth of children is also the most important Chinese and Japanese bodhisattva, Kwan-yin (Kannon in Japan), who assumed the attributes of the male bodhisattva of compassion, Avalokiteshvara, rather than

serving as his companion, like Tara. It was said that Kwan-yin filled the first ears of rice with milk from her breasts, pressing them until the last few drops were of blood rather than milk (which explains why rice may be both white and red). She—or rather the Buddha with whom she is linked, Amitabha—appears to have appropriated Hsi Wang Mu's western paradise (called the "pure land" in Chinese and Japanese Buddhism). Thus Kwan-yin is shown wearing a crown in which Amitabha's image is pre-eminent, seated on a lotus throne and holding the flaming jewel which symbolizes the enlightenment granted by the Buddhist law. In Japan, she has associations with water, and may be shown riding a fish or dolphin, but she has many incarnations, including that of Bato, when she has a horse's head. Perhaps her most popular form is that of Senju Kannon, "Kannon with a thousand hands," each of which is outstretched to help people. Although she may appear as a helper in a cloud of cherry-blossom petals, she has specific images which, like some of those proper to Virgin Mary, are believed to have miraculous

Mount Nariai that she transformed into food for a famished monk.

Numerous goddesses are worshipped within the indigenous Japanese Shinto tradition, such as Benten (equated with the Hindu Sarasvati), goddess of learning, love and sea, who is one of the seven Shichi Fukujin deities of good fortune. She is represented riding a dragon (or serpent) and holding a bow, arrow, wheel, sword and key in five of her eight hands. Inari, the deity of rice, is an ambivalent goddess (sometimes regarded as male), who is considered not only a benevolent bringer of food, but may have a trickster aspect when she takes the form of the fox, which is otherwise regarded as her messenger. A number of mountain goddesses are also worshipped, paramount among whom is Sengen-Sama, the goddess of Japan's most sacred mountain, Fujiyama, which some believe to be the cosmic mountain, or "navel" of the world,

attributes: the copper statue in Nigatsu-Do, for example, which may become as warm as a human body, or the wooden figure on

Left: Just as the traits of Avalokiteshiva were transferred to Kannon in Japan, so the bodhisattva Samantabhadra was transformed into Fugen-Bosatsu. **Below:** *As in other religious traditions, mountains have symbolic significance in the Far East: not only are they sacred to the particular deity that inhabits them, but they may also be equated with the cosmic mountain and the nurturing breasts of the Goddess.*

and goddess Izanami ("she who is invited"). It is told that her parents stood on either side of the Milky Way to churn the primeval ocean with a jeweled spear, thus creating the island Onogorojima, to which they descended. Izanami gave birth to all the features of earth, as well as the deities: Amaterasu (said to be created either from her mother's menstrual blood or from the left eye of her father), Tsuki-Yumi (the moon god), Susanowo (the storm god), and Kagu-Tsuchi (the fire god whose birth killed his mother). After her death, Izanami descended to the underworld, Yomi, to which Izanagi followed her, but, horrified by her corpse-like appearance, fled. Her creative function thus accomplished, Izanagi remained in the darkness of the underworld, but her daughter, by contrast, became "the great deity who illuminates heaven." Indeed, so radiant was she that her parents sent her up to the sky to illuminate the earth, her father giving her a necklace as a symbol of her rulership of the heavens.

Amaterasu was a sensitive goddess: first her brother and intended husband, Tsuki-Yumi, displeased her, so she banished him to the night sky; then she was upset by the noise and disruption that Susanowo created. When he flung a piebald colt into her weaving hall (for Amaterasu was a skilled weaver, and taught the art to humans) thereby killing her weaving maiden, Amaterasu retreated to a quiet cave (a symbol of the mother goddess) to sulk, sealing it with a boulder and thus removing her life-giving light and heat from the world. The lesser deities determined that she must be enticed from her hideaway if the earth was to be saved, and hatched a plan accordingly. The god of wisdom, Omoigane-no-kami, decided that the sakaki tree should be

Above: The rooster's ruddy plumage and habit of crowing at dawn associate it with the sun, and in Shinto belief, white cocks enticed Amaterasu from her cave. Thus the bird is an attribute of the solar goddess and kept at her shrines. The dragon is a sign of divine imperial authority. *Right:* The life-giving power of the Goddess is evoked in this Japanese icon of vegetation.

containing a cauldron that holds the water of life. Sengen is the guardian of this water, and is perceived as a beautiful young woman associated with the flower—whether a white camellia (*tsubaki*), anemone (*okina*), or wisteria (*fuji*)—that is her primary symbol.

The most important of the Japanese goddesses, Amaterasu, is unusual not only in the supreme position accorded to her but in her identification as a sun, rather than a moon, goddess. She is the daughter of the god Izanagi

uprooted and placed in front of the cave: on it they hung a mirror, beads and cloth. Then they created a commotion that caused the cocks to crow as if it were dawn. However, it was the lascivious dance of Ame-no-uzume ("alarming female of heaven," the deity of merriment and dancing) that aroused so much laughter that Amaterasu peeped from her cave to ask what all the noise was about. Ame-no-uzume answered that they had found a greater goddess than the sun goddess, and indicated the mirror. Amaterasu could not resist inspecting the object and hesitantly left her cave, whereupon Tajikara-no-mikoto, the god of strength, hauled her out of the darkness and the cave was sealed with a *shimenawa* rope to prevent her returning to it.

Thus Amaterasu's most important symbols are her necklace of solar sovereignty, the mirror (Yata Kagami) that reflects her radiance, and the cocks that herald her daily rising, (the birds are allowed to roam

around Shinto shrines.) Branches of the sakaki tree, banded by a white streamer, are also venerated today; *shimenawa* barricades still separate sacred sites; and Ame-no-uzume's dance continues to be re-enacted at Amaterasu's main shrine at Ise. Yet her symbols also have a more profound significance to the Japanese as the attributes of their ancestress. It is believed that Amaterasu's descendant was Jimmu-Tenno, the first Japanese emperor, and that, as a symbol of his sovereignty, she gave him the Yata Kagami, the sacred beads and the sword (Kusanagi-no-tsurugi) that Susanawo had wrested from the eight-tailed dragon. These three items are venerated as the imperial regalia, and their profound links with their divine bestower explain why, until after World War II, the Japanese emperor himself was regarded as a god. Since all Japanese people are considered cousins, Amaterasu is celebrated as the ancestress of all those to whom the Land of the Rising Sun is home.

Above: The radiant Amaterasu emerges at last from the cave where she had secluded herself, plunging the world into darkness. Her necklace represents her rulership of the heavens, and she bears the Kusanagi-no-tsurugi sword. Both symbols are part of Japanese imperial regalia. Left: This magnificent kimono is decorated with the vegetal motifs associated with the mother goddess. Bamboo represents devotion, while the chrysanthemum signifies happiness and longevity; it is also the national flower of Japan, since its shape recalls the sun.

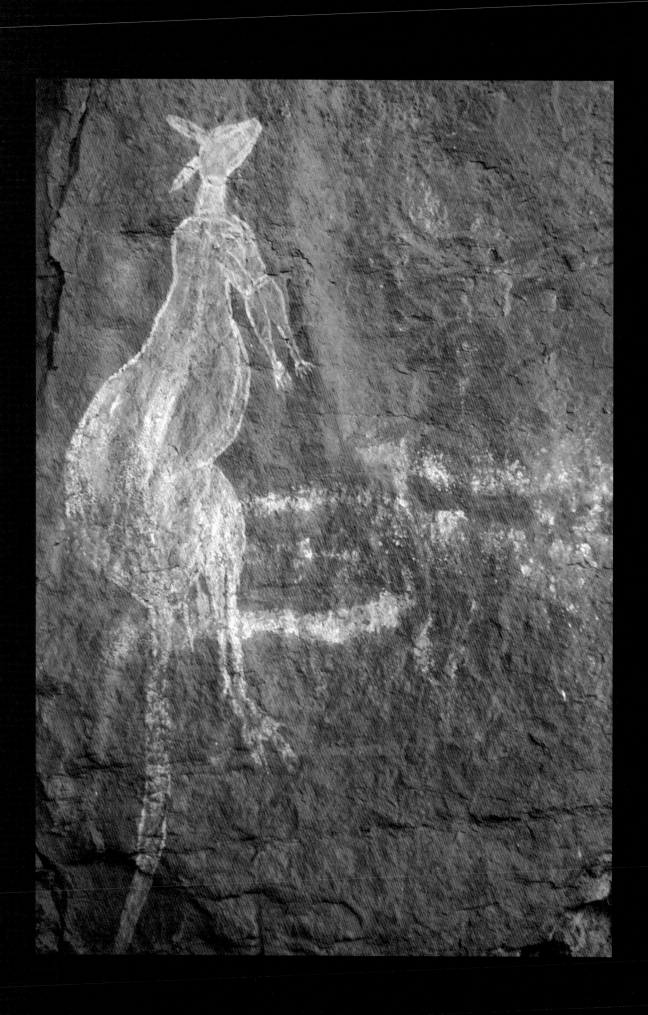

The Indigenous Cultures of Africa and the Pacific

Unlike most Western societies, the indigenous cultures of Africa, Australia, Polynesia and Melanesia remain firmly rooted in sacred traditions that have endured remarkably unchanged over the millennia. Although these ancient beliefs differ in detail, their fundamental elements are astonishingly similar despite their geographical disparity. Moreover, they have parallels in most of the world's earliest-documented civilizations. Not only do these lands share creation myths in which the Goddess plays a crucial role, but the tribal societies to which their people belong generally acknowledge a totemic ancestry leading back to the creator deity, a living link symbolized by the particular creature or plant that each regards as sacred to it. Therefore the Goddess manifests herself in the components of the natural world, be they serpents, fish, spiders or rice. Thus in these indigenous societies living in harmony with nature, the Goddess retains the function of which she was deprived by more complex societies. As the supreme provider of fertility, simultaneous giver and preserver of life, her continuing co-operation must be secured by means of ritual and prescribed behavior.

THE AFRICAN GODDESS

In common with the Celtic traditions of Northern Europe, the hundreds of African tribes have communicated their sacred concepts orally, as well as artistically, since ancient times. However, unlike the Celts, whose traditions were largely subsumed within the Christian faith, those of Africa are still handed down and celebrated by each successive generation. Given the local diversity of sacred beliefs across the continent, it is dangerous to generalize, or to identify any particular concept as being generically "African." However, some broad themes appear to characterize the basis upon which many traditions are founded: for instance, most believe that there is a single, relatively distant, supreme being, who presides over a multitude of lesser deities who have specific functions or localities. Individual and tribal ancestors are regarded as remaining actively interested in the affairs of their descendants, and it is these more tangible and personal entities who receive pleas for intercession and for benevolent treatment. Although the most powerful means of placating ancestors and divinities is by collective tribal rituals and the observance of significant rites of passage, supernatural power may also be contained in certain objects, such as fetishes, by which individuals may seek to

Opposite: Detail from an Australian Aboriginal rock painting of a kangaroo. Below: A Congolese carving of a mother and child. Background: The fish, a sign of fertility.

Background: *Hairstyles related to marriage rites among the Fanti, including two styles emulating cattle horns.* **Below:** *The Ashanti people of Ghana believe that the gift of fertility that the Goddess can confer is embodied in such artefacts as this beautifully carved figure.*

influence the direction of their lives. Similarly, the power of such goddesses as Aquaba, the Ashanti goddess of Ghana who is believed to make women fertile, may be stored within their images.

African mythology abounds with tales of twins, who may be accredited with the role of culture heroes but are sometimes also regarded as creator deities. Thus although some tribes believe that a single supreme being, either male or female, or even an androgynous entity (this uncertainty arising from the fact that many African languages dispense with the pronouns that identify gender) was responsible for creating the universe, many accord this role to a twin brother and sister. Among the Fon of Benin, for instance, the supreme deity, Mawu, is variously considered male, female, an androgynous being, or the female twin of the masculine Lisa. According to one version of the myth, Mawu and Lisa are the children of the demiurge Nanu Buluku (either female, or a hermaphrodite), who subsequently withdrew from the world. Mawu is the mature moon goddess, under whose refreshing and gentle light humans congregate, relax and communicate, recovering from the heat of the day that they have endured under the influence of Lisa, the sun god. The twins once united during an eclipse and gave birth to seven more sets of twins, including the sky goddesses Aizu and Akazu, who are also the deities of wealth; Ayaba, the goddess of the home and food; Naete, the sea goddess; and Gbadu, goddess of fate; each is symbolized by the attributes of her sphere of influence. Therefore, Mawu is worshipped as a mother goddess associated with the pleasurable aspects of the night in such a fiercely hot

climate: the passing on of wisdom, the pleasure of rest, and, of course, the procreation of children. Her primary symbol is the moon, but she may also be represented by the white fowl and goats that are sacrificed to her.

Almost everywhere, the earth is believed to be the body of the Goddess, and she is worshipped as both the mother who gives and sustains life, and as the underworld deity to whose womb the dead return. This concept is well illustrated among the Akan people of Ghana, who worship Asase Yaa ("Earth Thursday") as mother earth; since Thursday is sacred to her, no agricultural work may be performed on this day. In addition, her body is held in such respect that before the earth is disturbed, she must be placated: in spring, for example, a chicken is sacrificed to her before seeds are planted, and a libation is poured upon the ground before a grave is dug. The Ibo of Nigeria venerate Ala as the earth mother and regulator of life. In the many sculptures carved in homage to her, she is represented surrounded by children and grasping a knife fashioned from a yam—a dual symbol of life and death. In the Owerri region, Mbari houses are erected in Ala's honor at the prompting of a sign (such as the appearance of a snake) that she gives her priest. Built in a square form (an earth symbol), with one side left open, they contain figures fashioned of mud and painted in colorful hues of Ala, her children, and many other forms of life. Ala herself may again be depicted as cradling a child and holding a knife or dagger.

The observance of many rites of passage are also derived from the mythological stories associated with mother earth. The Dogon people of

them. That of the opposite sex is said to be excised by circumcision, thus removing any sexual ambiguity.

Unsurprisingly, water is also the realm of the African Goddess. The Dinka people of the Sudan, for example, regard Abuk, the wife of the first man, Garang, as a goddess associated with streams, so she is represented as a snake. Because she ground the first grains of corn, she is also the goddess of agriculture and therefore of the women who perform such work. The Yoruba people of Nigeria celebrate two water goddesses in particular: Oya and Oshun. Oya is the personification of the River Niger, and is symbolized as a rainbow serpent or a rainbow (as is Bunzi, the goddess of the Woyo people of Zaire and Dan, the female deity venerated by the

Left: Representations of the African Goddess emphasize her significance as the bringer of fertility, as seen in this idealized female form from the Ivory Coast. **Below:** *This finely executed detail from a Tassilli rock painting illustrates the importance of cattle within many tribal cultures. Such paintings may be regarded as devotional requests to the Goddess to bless her worshippers with abundance, since cattle are a form of wealth.*

Mali, for example, tell how their creator god, Amma, wished to have children with mother earth, but found his way barred by a red anthill (symbolizing the clitoris) which he was forced to destroy (this is regarded as the justification for the practice of female circumcision). A jackal was born, followed by male and female twins, the Nummo, who took the hybrid form of humans with snakelike nether regions. The Nummo clothed their naked mother with a skirt made of sacred fibers, simultaneously granting her the powers of speech. The perfidious jackal was jealous of this facility and, despite the fact that his mother changed herself into an ant and fled to an anthill (in this instance a womb symbol, as well as that of the cosmic mountain), it seized the fiber skirt and in so doing violated the goddess. Thus Amma felt obliged to create humans without her assistance, the Nummo giving each individual both male and female souls so that humans would have something of the twins within

Right: An antelope spirit mask from the Ivory Coast which, it is believed, will bestow its characteristics on the wearer. The antelope's grace and elusive speed link it symbolically to supernatural powers, including the goddess Coti, who is venerated by the Bushmen.

Far right: A Laonga woman carries her child on her back while tilling the soil. Agriculture, traditionally the sphere of women, confirms the natural link between motherhood, the earth and the Goddess.

Right: Masks like this one from Nigeria, which portrays a maiden spirit, are ritual objects believed to have transforming power—to endow their human wearers with the supernatural abilities and characteristics of the deity personified.

Mahis of Benin), for she can both cause rainstorms and restore meteorological order. Oshun, on the other hand, is the less energetic goddess of fresh water (who is especially associated with her eponymous river) and is therefore considered a goddess of healing as well as fertility. It is told that Oshun taught the gods the art of divination using the cowrie shells that are her attributes, along with fish. Many other goddesses are believed to possess the gift of prophecy: the Lango of Uganda, for example, regard the banyan tree as the oracle of Atida. While the serpent is a primary symbol of the Goddess, many other creatures are closely associated with a female deity: the Bushmen regard Coti as the mother of the antelope; Anansi is the clever spider goddess of Ghana; the Maguzawu people of Nigeria respect the hippopotamus as a manifestation of the goddess of the hunt; while the Senufus of the Ivory Coast wear crane masks during their rituals to bring them closer to Kono, the ancestress who assumes this form. Indeed, in most African cultures, masks may be donned during sacred rites to harness the power of the Goddess, and at least one goddess— Bayanni, who is venerated by the Yoruba of Nigeria—is solely ceremonial, embodied in the ritual casque headpiece that is studded with cowrie shells.

It is not only goddesses who are regarded as having supernatural powers—ancestresses, too, are accorded great respect, especially if they are divine queens. Clearly, in such a dry continent, rain is of the utmost importance in maintaining the earth's fertility, and this vital significance is reflected in the hierarchy of the Luvedu people of the Transvaal, whose hereditary (mortal) rain queen is known as Mujaji. Legend tells that the original possessor of her rain-making powers was a princess of Zimbabwe, who fled her homeland for the Transvaal after giving birth to an illegitimate son, taking her father's rain charm and the associated sacred beads with her. One of her descendants was King Mugodo, who, as a result of an incestuous relationship with his daughter, Mujaji, had a daughter, also named Mujaji. The first Mujaji was unambiguously associated with the moon, for she was also called "one who gives water," "white-faced one," and "radiant as the sun." It was during the reign of her daughter, however, that the Luvedu territory was invaded by both Europeans and Zulus, as a result of which Mujaji II committed suicide. It is still believed that if disaster befalls the tribe, or if the rain queen becomes ill, she must end her life in order to pass her powers on to a younger woman better able to perform them. The attributes of these Luvedu rain queens are secret, but it is believed that they include the original rain charm and beads, as well as the skins of their ancestors and sacred "rain pots." Just as the Moombi people of Kenya celebrate their eponymous ancestress ("the molder"), Bwayla Chabala is venerated by her Bemba descendants in Zambia by placing flour and cloth in a basket that was said to belong to her. This symbolic offering of food and clothing is made at the shrine erected over her grave in a direct request for her favor.

As a result of the forcible transportation of innumerable African people across the Atlantic as slaves, many African deities enjoy a devoted following in the Americas in the form of the *loas* (gods) of Voodoo. Reflecting the different cultures and faiths to which the erstwhile slaves were exposed, Voodoo is today a richly syncretic blend of sacred beliefs in which those of West Africa are prominent. To give examples, the Ghanaian spider goddess, Anansi, became the rather more prosaically named Aunt Nancy, and we also re-encounter the Nigerian water goddesses Oya and Oshun in the West Indies. The latter's Puerto Rican symbol is the pumpkin, whose numerous seeds represent fertility and wealth. Oya is also associated with the Guede, Voodoo death spirits, and she takes the form of Brigitte, the guardian of the cemeteries, in Haiti. Erzulie is one of Voodoo's most important sea *loas*, and she may be identified with Aziri, the goddess who is worshipped by the Fon of Benin; in her Voodoo context, this goddess personifies love and beauty, but also jealousy. She is regarded as the mistress of many gods: when associated with Legba, god of the crossroads and magic, it is said that her moon-white skin is tanned by his heat. She is enticed into Voodoo temples, or *hounfours*, by the drawing of her symbol (*vêve*)—a heart—upon the floor, and, upon manifesting herself, will beautify herself and flirt with her worshippers. Like many water goddesses, Erzulie may be personified and revered as a snake, but perhaps the most important such serpent *loa* is Aida-Wedo (equated with the African Mawu), the rainbow serpent who is the consort of Danbhalah-Wedo, the creator god.

Left: In Puerto Rico, the many-seeded pumpkin—a symbol of fruitfulness—is associated with the Voodoo goddess Oshun, whose worship was imported to the Caribbean from Africa by Nigerian slaves. *Below:* A wooden box from Guinea in the form of a hippopotamus. Many African tribes, including the Nigerian Maguzuwa people, venerate this creature for its strength, fecundity and affinity with water, all qualities associated with the Goddess. *Background:* A heart, symbolic of the Voodoo goddess Erzulie.

Above: A wondjina *figure from the sacred art of Kimberley, Western Australia.* **Below:** *For Aborigines, Ayers Rock, or Uluru, in the Northern Territory, is a sacred site inhabited by spirits of the Dreaming.*

THE AUSTRALIAN GODDESS

Rainbow serpents are also an important manifestation and symbol of the Goddess in the Aboriginal cultures of Australia. Despite the diversity of their tribal mythologies, and the varying significance that they accord their respective totemic spirits, all Aborigines trace the dawning of the cosmos to a period called the Dreamtime, or Dreaming, when the first beings emerged from the primal sea and wandered about on the dry land, creating geographical features (frequently from parts of their bodies), as well as animals, birds, plants, fish and humans, and also establishing the tribal customs that are still observed. Many tribes, like those of the Kimberley area, believe that these ancient ancestors—*wondjina*—are still involved in their welfare and may bestow the gift of rain or fertility in response to the "increase rituals" that their human descendants perform. The *wondjina* are personified in the sacred rock art of Western Australia as ghostlike figures surrounded by elements of the natural world; many Aborigines believe that these images were created by the *wondjina* themselves, who continue their existence within such topographical features as Ayer's Rock.

The Dreamtime mythologies of Arnhem Land tell the story of Kunapipi ("old woman"/"mother"), the rainbow serpent whose daughters (the Munga Munga) lure men into her lair so that she can eat them. During male initiation rites, boys are told that they will be swallowed and then regurgitated into adult life by the rainbow serpent. This tale is paralleled in the beliefs of Northern Australia, where the primeval serpent Karawadi ("mother of all," also known as Mutjingga, the ogress) ate several children; she was tracked down by their parents who slit open her body to reveal their children, who were then reborn. During initiation rites, blood-daubed boys are placed in a cave or waterhole (womb symbols) to be swallowed and reborn to the accompaniment of the voice of the goddess, believed to be incarnated in the sound of the bullroarer. Such rainbow serpents as Ngaljod, the daughter of Yingarna (the mother rainbow serpent) also play an important role in the female rites that mark puberty: to mark the occasion of her first menstrual period, the girl is smeared with red ocher (representing blood), while either a crescent moon or Ngaljod's rainbow-serpent symbol (interchangeable in symbolic terms) is drawn between her breasts. Other rainbow serpents include Eingana, who is worshipped by the Djauan clan; it is said that she holds the string of life attached to the heels of all living creatures, and death results when she relinquishes it. Most Australian Aboriginal societies believe that waterholes (which, like the Celtic wells, are considered passageways to the underworld) are inhabited by rainbow serpents that must not be disturbed lest, as in the case of Narama's lair in the Liverpool River, she is angered by the intrusion and kills those who have awakened her by drowning or swallowing them.

Other Dreamtime stories speak of the two Djanggawul sisters, who created natural features, particularly freshwater lakes, with their digging sticks during their primal perambulations, giving birth to the first humans on conical mats (symbols of the cosmic mountain). Their brother, envious of his siblings' procreative powers, stole their sacred dillybags in an attempt to appropriate their abilities for himself, but the sisters remained pre-eminent, for they alone could give birth. They are symbolized aniconically by rounded shapes arranged roughly in the form of a cross, which together represent the lakes they created and the routes that they travelled between them, while their digging sticks are believed to have taken root as trees. Another pair of sisters, the Jungoka, created both waterholes and aquatic creatures; in their case, the powers embodied in their digging sticks were successfully stolen by their sons.

The main incarnation of the Australian Goddess, therefore, is in the form of the rainbow serpent. However, she may also be a sun goddess (the moon is always associated with a male deity in Aboriginal belief). Such deities include the goddess Alinga, venerated by the Arunta people; Gnowee, who illuminates the earth with a torch in search of her son; Wuriupranala, who covers her body with red ocher; or Dinewan, who takes the form of an emu and whose egg is the globe of sun. Goddesses who assume the guise of birds include another emu goddess, Kalaia; her sister, Kipara, a turkey; Bima, who, after the death of her child was transformed into the curlew whose cry expresses her grief; and Brogla, who accompanies tribal dancers in the form of a bird. Another bird

goddess is Parabaruma, who was beaten by her suitor, Yurumu, and changed herself into the masked plover, whose pain-filled cry and loosely hanging red skin recall her distress. Other animals associated with goddesses include Minmawaiuda, the possum woman; Naruni, mother of the duck-billed platypus; and the frog goddess Kwouk Kwouk, whose daughters control the weather. All are both sacred symbols and totemic animals.

As in Africa, some tribes—particularly in central Australia—regard the protagonists of the Dreaming as beings who are now removed from the events of life. Customarily, people turn to their totemic ancestors, the offspring of the Dreamtime demiurges, for assistance. So important is the continuing presence of these ancestors that they are regarded as the parents of newborn children. It is said that their spirits enter the unborn fetus when its mother passes the particular feature of the land in which the ancestors sleep (men are still believed to play a negligible part in procreation). The goddess Anjea, for example,

Above: *This rock painting from Kakadu, Arnhem Land, in Australia's Northern Territory, represents Kunapipi, the mother of all things, giving birth. Her status as ancestral mother-goddess is shown by her many names, including "All Mother," "Old Woman" and "Fertility Mother."*
Background: *The kangaroo, who carries her young in her protective pouch, is sacred to Australian Aborigines.*

is thought to fashion babies from mud and then to place them in their mothers' wombs, while Minma-milbali contributes that part of the soul that connects the child to the Dreamtime. Such ancestors are symbolized by the creatures that are their totems, and which must therefore be treated respectfully: the emu, for example, is the emblem of the crow mother Kurikuta, who creates thunder and lightning if her sacred bird is eaten.

In the tribal rituals and, indeed, in the very way of life of the Australian Aborigines, the Goddess—as creator, preserver and destroyer—continues to regulate society. Through their rites and everyday actions, the people reflect and appease the power that she is believed to wield over them and regard themselves as living links in the chain that leads back to their primal creator.

Right: Many Aboriginal goddesses are symbolized by birds—including Dinewan and Kalaia, who take the form of emus— while their eggs are the visible manifestation of the power to create new life. Their ties to such goddesses endow creatures like the emu with profound sacred significance.

THE POLYNESIAN AND MELANESIAN GODDESS

The tribal cultures of Polynesia also cherish the totems bestowed upon them by their primal ancestors, but in many ways their creation myths are more akin to those of the ancient Mediterranean world than to those of Australia or Africa. Furthermore, parts of Polynesia—especially the Indonesian islands of Java and Bali—were exposed to Hinduism, with the result that such goddesses as Kali, Durga, Saraswati (who, in Bali, is symbolized by a lizard) and Uma are objects of veneration in these regions. Perhaps the most profound example of a Polynesian appropriation of a Hindu goddess is seen in the rituals devoted to the Indonesian Dewi Sri (Tisnawati in western Java). She is equated with Lakshmi (as Sita, "the furrow") and is widely worshipped as the mother of the most important staple crop—rice. At harvest, for example, the largest grain of rice (symbolizing the rice mother) is placed in the storage shed before the rest of the crop. While it is being stored, the vigilant concern of the rice mother is symbolized by the cat, who keeps hungry rodents at bay. In addition, the tallest stalks of rice are harvested first, and the "bridal couple" (equated with Vishnu and Lakshmi) are then anointed with oil and wrapped in a cloth before being placed in the rice shed, in the hope that they will procreate profusely.

The Polynesians also rejoice in a sophisticated indigenous mythology. One cosmogony tells that in the beginning was a chaotic primal vacuum, Mamao ("space"), which is regarded as a female entity paired with the masculine Ilu ("the firmament"). Together they created (the feminine) night, Po, and (the masculine) day, Ao. Another myth says that Po was the first mother (symbolized by the Milky Way), who gave birth to the sun, moon and stars, and then

Left: The Hindu goddess Durga, called "the unapproachable one," destroys the buffalo demon in this nineteenth-century painting. Hinduism spread from India to Polynesia: thus Durga is venerated in Bali and Java as the terrible goddess of death and disease, as well as of black magic. Indonesian folk art often displays a blend of indigenous and Hindu symbolism.

the *atua* (deities), the components of the natural world and, finally, humans. Her creative function accomplished, Po became the realm of darkness and death.

General Polynesian tradition (in which names and details vary), holds that although the first god was Tangaroa, the deity of the sea, the world's various features were created when Rangi (or Atea), the sky, coupled with Papa (rather confusingly, the name of mother earth). Since their embrace was so close, no light could penetrate the couple, which meant that nothing could grow. Thus they were eventually separated by their son, Tane, god of light and the forests, who took the form of a tree in performing this task (in this respect, the myth is astoundingly similar to that of ancient Greece concerning Gaia and Ouranos). Papa's sorrow at this forcible separation is said to manifest itself in the mistlike vapor that rises from the earth, while Rangi weeps rain from the sky. As in so many other sacred cultures, the body of Papa can therefore be regarded as the most important generative power, both creating and sustaining life.

The goddess Hine, or Hina, who has at least ninety documented aspects, is pre-

eminent among Polynesian goddesses: she is not only the deity of the moon and the ruler of Po, but has power over the waters and taught women such useful crafts as making cloth from tapa bark. As Hine-ahu-one she is the first woman, whom Tane fashioned from earth. Tane then took their daughter, Hine-i-tau-ira ("dawn maiden"), as his wife, but when she discovered that she had committed incest she fled to Po, where she is venerated as the death goddess, Hine-nui-te-po ("great Hine, the night"). It is told that Maui, the Maori culture hero, tried to cheat death by creeping through Hine's body unnoticed, but was trapped within her womb when she was awakened by a fantail: thus humans must inevitably die to return to her, and on their deathbeds might glimpse Hine's black form and green eyes. As the moon goddess, Hine also takes many forms: as Hina-Uri ("the indigo lady"), for example, she presides over the moon's dark phase and represents the dawning of new life, while as Hina-Keha ("bright lady") she is the goddess of the full moon who, it is told, once fell to earth and gave birth to a son by a mortal man. This myth explains why she is also regarded as a goddess of childbirth (who may be accompanied by a dog), and women may still chant the pain-relieving spell (*karakia*) that she was the first to utter when giving birth. As the moon, Hine also controls the tides and has close associations with the ocean: as Hine-Te-Ngaru-Moana, she takes the form of a mermaid, and as Hina-Ika is celebrated as the inventor of fishing nets, which she originally wove from the silver rays of her moon hair. Yet despite her primary association with the moon, death and water, Hine is also believed to be the goddess who rules such diverse natural forces as the west wind (Hine-tu-whenua), when she blows canoes to safety, or as the goddess of fire (Hine-i-tapeka). Indeed, so wide-ranging are her powers that Hine may be regarded as the greatest of Polynesian goddesses, even though in some traditions lesser deities are accorded her respective attributes, including Rona (the moon), Miru (the death goddess whose lovely daughters entice men to the underworld where she cooks them in her oven and eats them) and Ka'ipo (a water goddess).

Central to Polynesian sacred belief is the importance of maintaining *mana*—the spiritual power that flows downward from the realm of the deities to that of humans—which, if the required rituals are observed correctly and *tapus* (taboos) are not broken, will bring personal and tribal success. Many goddesses will vent their displeasure if such sacred conventions are not respected. And, as in Celtic mythology, there are instances of triple war goddesses, such as the granddaughters of Hine in her earth-goddess aspect (Hine-Tu-a-Uta), whom the Polynesians call Ai-Tuapuai ("head-eater"), Toi-Mata ("ax with eyes") and Mahu-Fatu-Rau ("escape from a hundred stones" or "frog of many owners"). One might venture the theory that while Polynesian sacred tradition does include some animal goddesses, such as the Hawaiian Mamala (a lizard, shark or crocodile woman) and the lizard woman Pi'i-ka-lalau, the principles,

features and symbols of the goddesses of Polynesian mythology appear to be more closely related in spirit to those of the early Western world than to the primarily totemic-based beliefs of Africa, Australia and Melanesia.

Although the many traditions of Melanesia share the Polynesian belief in *mana*, in common with the tribal mythologies and customs of Africa and Australia, the creator deities collectively known as the *demas* play a less immediate role in everyday life than do the *tumbuna*—totemic ancestors of the tribes—or the *masalai* spirits believed to inhabit natural features. Thus the primary importance of the Goddess as demiurge is in her creative actions, but other goddesses may promote her gift of fecundity. Prominent mother goddesses include, in New Guinea, Afekan, who is said to have created the world, also giving people pigs (symbols of prosperity) and taro plants and educating them in the correct rituals necessary to maintain natural fertility. After creating animals, Cassowary Mother's body gave vegetables

Right: Tahitian women painted by Paul Gauguin stand at the ocean's edge accompanied by a dog; both sea and animal are associated with the multifaceted goddess Hine, the female deity who has supreme importance in Polynesian sacred belief.
Background: *A hook in the form of a New Guinea goddess.*

Left: *The lives of the inhabitants of Polynesia's many islands are dominated by the sea around them: thus they venerate the goddesses who preside over this realm, including such lesser deities as Ka'ipo, as well as the pre-eminent Hine, the lunar goddess and controller of the tides.* **Background:** *The sow, an emblem of fertility.*

to the people, and her bones produced a staple food, the yam. Many Melanesian creator goddesses assume the familiar serpent form: in San Cristoval, for example, mythology tells of the snake goddess Kagauaha, who gave humans the gift of animals and other forms of food; the Solomon Islanders venerate Kahausibware and Koevasi, the latter regarded the mother of the first woman. In New Guinea, too, Toobunaygu is the goddess of snakes, while the python goddess Niniganni is believed to bestow good fortune and wealth on her worshippers. Such goddesses are important for their creative functions, but other female deities are believed to act as preservers of fertility if worshipped properly: in New Guinea, for example, Yam Woman, Sherok and Siniekili are all viewed as patrons of the yam, and the Bonito Maidens of the Solomon Islands as providers of the eponymous fish.

Some myths equate the "death" of the creator goddess with the underworld—in New Guinea, for instance, it is related that Hainuwele was murdered by mortal men, after which her body sprouted tubers and other vegetation. The goddess Satene ("judgement") was so outraged by her sister's murder that she retreated to the underworld, where she has stood ever since with her arms raised in an arch. If humans have led a virtuous life, she will allow them into her realm and might later grant them reincarnation in human form; if they have dis-

pleased her, however, they will be reborn as spirits or animals. Satene performs much the same function as did Ma'at in ancient Egyptian lore. Certain Melanesian goddesses (such as Hana, daughter of the mother goddess Honabe) are also considered lunar deities and share the nocturnal attributes of other traditions. Such goddesses as Makunai and Osooso, who are venerated as the mothers of the Eagle tribes of Bougainvillea and the Solomon Islands, may also be divine ancestors, symbolized by the totemic eagle. Such *tumbuna* spirits may communicate with their descendants through dreams and divination, and are sometimes believed to be embodied in sacred stones, as ancient European goddesses were in megaliths. In New Guinea, for example, the Dama goddesses (who may sometimes mate with mortal men) are symbolized by stones, as is Gauteaki in the Solomon Islands, who is also worshipped in this form on Bellona Island, along with Nguatupu'a, patroness of the Tanga tribe of the Bellona Islands.

Despite the remoteness of the islands comprising Melanesia, it is a significant reflection of the hold of the Goddess on the human psyche that the region's female deities equate clearly to the classic archetypal forms of the Goddess: earth mothers, tutelary deities, preservers of fertility, underworld and lunar deities—all are richly represented in Melanesia.

The Goddess of the Americas

The indigenous sacred beliefs of the Americas are characterized by remarkable diversity. It is estimated, for example, that there are still more than 200 Native American tribal groupings; moreover, since the integrity of most of them was profoundly affected by such external factors as migration and European incursions into their lands and cultures, their sacred beliefs have not remained static. Thus it is impossible to group this myriad of traditions into a conveniently homogeneous category. Despite this qualification, certain fundamental concepts can be said to underpin the mythologies and rituals of most indigenous American faiths, primarily the sanctity invested in the various components of the natural world—traditionally the domain of the Goddess. Reflecting this sacramental view of nature, the Goddess of the Americas is endowed with the primary significance accorded to her the world over—as the creator of life and maintainer of fertility. Tragically, some American cultures did not survive the European invasions, notably the Mesoamerican societies, with their complex pantheons of deities, mythologies and rituals. Within these now extinct sacred beliefs, the various universal manifestations of the Goddess and her symbols—among them, the serpent, vegetation, water, the moon and the earth—were richly represented, but are now known to us only through codices and artefacts. In the latter instance, it is perhaps the depiction of the agonized Coatlicue, the murdered, serpent-skirted mother goddess, which best symbolizes both the age-old value of the Goddess to the people and her devolution and destruction in modern times.

THE NATIVE AMERICAN GODDESS

In common with many other tribal societies, those of the Americas believe that humankind is an integral part of the natural world, neither separate from nor superior to it, but rather an inextricable link in the chain of life. This holistic view is completely compatible with all the principles represented by the Goddess as controller of the natural cycle of birth, death and rebirth. Humanity, it is taught, must respect and maintain the harmonious balance of nature, and one of the most effective ways of doing so is believed to be by means of tribal rituals. Because of the large number of Native American tribes, instead

Opposite: *The Navajo believe that Spider Rock, in Canyon de Chelly, Arizona, is the site from which Spider Woman spun the thread that gave life to humanity.*
Below: *This colorful Tlingit headdress dates from around 1800 and represents sea creatures. The symbolic images of the peoples of the Northwestern Coast are totemic, for the creatures depicted have sacred ancestral significance to the tribe.*

Right: The web that forms the center of the dream-catcher is believed to have the power to entangle and retain dreams and visions; this artefact is a primary symbol of Spider Woman.
Below: Besides serving a practical purpose for traditionally nomadic people, the basketwork produced by Navajo women is decorated with sacred motifs drawn from the tribe's legends. Many Native American peoples believe that crafts were originally taught to them by tutelary goddesses.
Background: The life-giving maize plant.

of examining the role of the Goddess within each, it is probably more meaningfully to categorize the types of goddesses venerated widely among the indigenous peoples. In so doing, it becomes clear that the Native American Goddess conforms to the archetypal forms that prevail everywhere—as creator, earth mother, moon goddess, totemic ancestress, and mistress of the animals—these roles frequently being interrelated.

Some Native American cosmogonies tell that the universe was formed by such female deities as the Spider Woman (or Sussistinnako, "Thought Woman") of the Pueblo tribes, who spun her web from each of the four cardinal directions to create the cosmos, and later made humans from clay. Other Pueblo traditions regard this goddess, also known as Gogyeng So Wuhti ("spider grandmother"), as the deity who led the first humans from the underworld (or the womb of mother earth) through the cracks in the surface to their

new home. Spider Woman's primary symbols include the dreamcatcher, whose net is equated with the web of life, and which is thought to entrap visions and thus influence fate. It is relatively rare, however, that the Goddess has such fundamental significance, since most Native American sacred beliefs give the role of cosmic creation to a male supreme deity. Yet despite the fact that goddesses are not often acknowledged as generators of the sun, moon and stars, for instance, they may play a more intimate—and, in many ways, more important—role in tribal mythology: as the facilitator of humanity's emergence onto the earth, as the provider of food, and as the establisher of sacred rituals.

The Goddess as earth mother features prominently in Native American sacred beliefs, for not only does she generate life, she also receives humans into her body after their deaths so that they may be at one with nature before their subsequent rebirths. So numerous are the Native American earth mothers that we can examine only a few. The Hopi, for example, believe that all terrestrial life was created by the union of mother earth and father sky. In the sacramental sand paintings (whose form is said to have been dictated by the deities, or *yeis*) created during the related Navajo ceremonies of ritual and renewal, mother earth may be depicted in association with a spring of life-giving water and with plants sprouting from her body. The Navajo especially celebrate Eshtanatlehi, or Changing Woman, for it was she who—with her consort, the sun— gave life to the Navajo hero twins and then made the first humans. After filling two baskets with white and yellow flour, she shook dead, scaly skin from her breasts,

and added water to make a paste from which she modeled man (from the white-flour mixture) and woman (from the yellow). Changing Woman eventually settled in the West, but not before she had provided humans with creatures and plants; she now changes her form according to the seasons, and is represented only in the sand paintings that accompany the Blessingway ceremony. Nokomis, too, is regarded as the nourisher of all life by the Algonquian nation. Nokomis is called "Grandmother" because this was her relationship with the Algonquian culture-hero twins, Nanabuth, the Great Hare, and Chibiabos, the Wolf. It is told that the underworld serpents murdered Chibiabos, whose brother later avenged his death and then forced the serpents to instruct him and Nokomis in the art of using healing herbs, and in the pattern of the Midewiwin or Medicine Dance that prolongs life. The Cheyenne, whose most important sources of food were the bison herds and maize, celebrate the bringer of this largesse as Old Woman (or Bison Woman). After she was

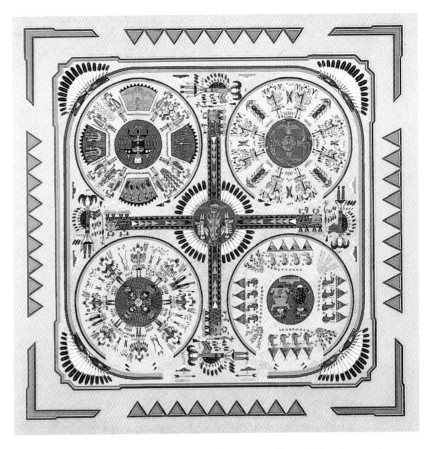

discovered in the bowels of a hill (symbolizing both the cosmic mountain and the womb of the mother goddess) by two

Above: Navajo sand, or dry, paintings are created for a specific ritual healing ceremony and then destroyed immediately afterward. The form of these paintings was believed to have been taught by the yeis—the Navajo spirits—whose curative powers are symbolically harnessed by their images. *Left:* A sixteenth-century illustration of Native Americans sowing corn and beans in Florida. While men prepare the ground, women sow the seeds, for it is the Goddess rather than a male deity who is traditionally especially associated with cereal crops.

Above: A Tsuu T'ina
woman dries meat over
a fire in Alberta, Canada.
In many systems of Native
American sacred belief,
women were first taught
such practical arts by
benevolent tutelary
female spirits.

her lodge and saw the divine women's sacred dance, during which Evening Star Woman (the planet Venus) held the moon in her basket while the four daughters of Big Black Meteor Star (the deity of magic who advises medicine men)—all bearing two white swans' necks and fawn skins (lunar fertility symbols) in their baskets—danced to the west, finally offering their baskets to Evening Star Woman. These stellar deities taught the first Pawnee couple to make a basket lined with mud—symbolizing creation—and presented them with twelve branches (representing the Pleiades). It is Evening Star Woman rather than Moon Woman who is regarded as the creator of natural features. She is also the mother of First Woman by Morning Star, who taught her tribe language, ritual and agricultural practices; to this day sacred Pawnee decorative patterns include a map of the stars. Many other tribes regard the moon as a feminine entity: one of the forms that the Navajo Changing Woman may assume, for example, is that of Yolkai Estan ("white shell woman"), when she is also regarded as a moon goddess, whose symbol is the abalone shell. Yet among some tribes, and also in the Arctic region, the moon is believed to be a male god, whose solar sister (called Akycha among the Inuit) chases him across the sky; both carry torches, but hers is brighter than his.

young men swimming upstream, she presented the intruders with two pots containing bison meat and maize, from which they magically fed their tribe until the supply was exhausted. Since then, bisons have been generated by the spring and maize by the fields. Thus Old Woman is closely linked in mythological terms to the goddesses of northern Europe, who share her symbols of life-giving water, cosmic mountains and cauldrons of abundance, as well as creatures of the hunt and corn.

Although she may not be the supreme deity, the moon goddess also plays an important part in Native American mythology and ritual. The Pawnee, for instance, tell of Moon Woman, whose daughters by the sun were the stars. The first Pawnee boy and girl happened upon

One of the most important natural manifestations of the Goddess is as a deity of corn—the principal cereal crop of the Americas. The Native Americans of the Plains, for instance, tell that the supreme (male) deity, Nezaru, created maize, whose seeds germinated into the first humans. Spiders were then sent below the earth to procreate, thus creating giants (whom Nezaru drowned in a flood) and animals. Next Nezaru sent Corn Mother from his heavenly cornfields to this subterranean realm; she thrust herself through the earth toward the light and led the animals and humans to the West. She taught her people how to cultivate maize and how to worship the deities. It was she who gave humans the components of their sacred medicine bundles, instructed the women in the art of the game of shinny, and told the tribes to smoke tobacco in veneration of the gods of the eight directions. Her task accomplished, Corn Mother returned to the sky, leaving behind her the cedar tree by which she is remembered, as well as the maize. During the elaborate annual rituals of the Zuñis, when they believe that the *kachinas* (or *kokos,* the spirits of vegetation, animals and human ancestors) have returned to the tribe, women represent various aspects of the *kachinas.* Corn Maidens manifest themselves during the Molawai ceremony wearing the various costumes of the maize plant; Tukwinong Mana ("cumulus cloud kachina maiden") carries a tray of maize of four different colors during the Shalako festival; and Ahmetolela Okya ("rainbow dancer girl") dances among the people, all wearing masks and clothing specific to their roles. Among the Hopi, too, such *kachinas* as A-ha Kachin' Mana, the bean *kachina* that appears during the Powamu bean dance, or Poli Kachina Mana ("butterfly girl"), represent the vital forces of nature whose cooperation the tribe seeks to enlist.

Thus the Goddess may be regarded as a tutelary spirit, who in ancient times instructed her people on how to conduct their lives, and gave them the symbolic totems (such as medicine bundles) that serve as a constant reminder of their sacred obligations. The most venerated totemic symbol of the Sioux, for instance, is the peace pipe, or calumet, that they received from White Buffalo Woman, who entered their midst with the words: "I came from heaven to teach the Sioux how to live . . . I give you this pipe. Keep it always." This envoy then instructed the tribe in the pipe-smoking ritual, and taught other sacred rites (including the White Buffalo Ceremony and the Sun Dance) that are still observed. After presenting them with four grains of maize, she finally departed, transforming herself into a buffalo: "I am a buffalo, the White Buffalo Cow. I will spill my milk all over the earth, that the people may live." The ritual smoking of the calumet is a sacred act among many Plains tribes, for the smoke that wafts upward is believed to be a form of communion with the supernatural world. The pipe itself may be regarded as a cosmic symbol: its clay bowl representing the earth; its wooden stem, vegetation; and its carved decorative motifs, birds and animals; while the tobacco may be equated with humankind.

Left: This Adena pipe in the form of a human figure dates from Ohio's Mound Culture era, and was made between 800 and 100 BC. Calumets are sacred ritual objects in Native American belief: smoking them enables human communion with the deities.

Below: A California Klamath cave painting, packed with symbols that are believed to relate to stars and their movements. Many Native American goddesses are equated with astral bodies.

Above and below: Tribes of the Northwestern Pacific Coast accord enormous significance to such totemic ancestors as the Tlingit Bear Mother. By donning this bear mask for rituals, the wearer is believed to assume the characteristics of the spirit symbolized. Totemic creatures represented on the painted Nootka board (1800) include a serpent, thunderbird and whale.
Background: Inuit carving of a woman/fish creature.

Goddesses may also be associated with specific totemic creatures, whose lives are respected by the tribe. Among the Iroquois, for example, the killing of eagles has been prohibited ever since a hunter was abducted by Mother of All Eagles in punishment for his murder of her offspring, motivated by his desire for their feathers. He lured the eagles within range with deer meat and then shot them. While he tied up her fledglings' beaks, Mother of All Eagles was forced to release him, but not before he had promised to spare her kind in future. The Tlingits venerate the Bear Mother, originally a human princess who married a bear that was later killed by her outraged clan. Its descendants may harness the help of their primal father by wearing his skin. Tlingit house screens are decorated with the symbol of the brown-bear mother in homage to their ancestry, while the totem poles that proclaim their identity and beliefs may also display her image prominently.

While Native American goddesses are closely linked to the bounty of the earth in all its forms, among the Arctic and Subarctic peoples, the Goddess is associated more closely with the sea, which she rules as mistress of marine life. This sea goddess has various names, but all correspond to the Inuit Sedna. There are many myths relating to Sedna: one says that she was the insatiably hungry daughter of two giants who began to eat her parents while they slept. Her parents awoke and (not surprisingly) resolved to get rid of their daughter. They rowed her out to sea and pushed her out of their boat; however, Sedna clung desperately to the sides, forcing her father to release her grip by chopping off her fingers, which became seals, walruses, whales and fish. Sedna finally sank to the seabed where, it is said, she now lives, directing the migration of her aquatic offspring and causing storms at sea when angry. Indeed, she is a temperamental and capricious goddess, who demands devoted worship in return for her favors. Shamans (*angakoks*) still call upon this great sea mother for guidance when famine threatens their people.

THE MESOAMERICAN GODDESS

Despite their worshippers, few of the indigenous goddesses of Central and South America survived the brutal incursion of the European *conquistadores* into their lands during the fifteenth and sixteenth centuries, the most spectacular casualties being those of Mesoamerica (2300 BC to AD 1521). The Aztec system of sacred belief that was destroyed in 1521 was founded upon the influential religious traditions of the Mayans—a maize-growing people who not only developed a remarkably accurate calendrical system in an attempt to exert control over the agricultural cycle, but who also gave their deities ultimate responsibility for the earth's fertility. Many of their complicated sacred rituals were conducted at temples built on top of huge stepped pyramids—symbols of the cosmic mountain. Like their successors, the Mayans conceived of thirteen hierarchies

of sky deities—bestowers of fertility— who were in constant opposition with their rivals of the nine levels of the underworld, the bringers of death. Despite this distinction, it should be noted that all Mesoamerican deities had both benevolent and destructive sides to their natures.

Although most of the significant Mayan gods were regarded as masculine, including the creator deity, Itzamna, one of the pre-eminent deities was female: the moon goddess, Ix Chel ("lady rainbow," a title shared with her daughter, Chibilias), the consort of Izamna and also of Ah Kin, the god of the sun. In common with most Mesoamerican goddesses, Ix Chel was an ambivalent mother figure. On the one hand, she taught women such useful arts as healing, divination and weaving (a tutelary function continued by her lunar daughter, Ix Chebel Yax) and was the patroness of childbirth and magic; on the other, she could influence the tides so as

Above: After the destruction of Mesoamerican sacred traditions by the Spanish during the sixteenth century, little remained of the highly developed Mayan civilization apart from the ancient monuments in Yucatan.

*Right: The Mayan gods of Mesoamerica were depicted by means of an elaborate symbolic language, as seen in these stone carvings from Yucatan. Mayan worship centered on a complex mythology of the underworld and cosmic regeneration. **Below:** This earth-mother figure, portrayed in the birth-giving position, was created by a craftsman of the Taino people, another Mesoamerican civilization whose sacred beliefs were extinguished with their adherents.*

to cause flooding and death. There has been some argument among scholars as to whether Ix Chel was regarded as a youthful and beautiful goddess ("Goddess I" in the codices) or as an aged crone ("Goddess O" or Chac Chel). The former was depicted with the claws of an eagle and wearing a feathered headdress, and was accompanied by a screech owl (a symbolic bringer of rain and a messenger from the underworld), while Chac Chel was a fearsome hag who sported jaguar claws and had serpents writhing in her hair. In terms of the generic Goddess, however, this academic dispute is somewhat irrelevant, for, as we have seen, both these representations are aspects of the Goddess and are not, therefore, incompatible.

The chief Mayan goddesses associated with the moon were closely linked with water, as well as with wisdom, fertility and crafts. Some of these associations may be underlined by the names and functions of many lesser goddesses, in whom demi-animal forms indicate the creature that symbolized them, including Ix Chancab ("the female snake-bee"), Ix Kan Citam Thul ("she, the precious peccary rabbit,"—simultaneously a lunar symbol and an animal that was hunted), Ix Tol Och ("she, the big-bellied possum") and Ix Ual Cuy ("she, the horned owl of extended wings"). Ix Tub Tan was said to be a snake who spat out jewels (raindrops). Certain Mayan goddesses also presided over death,

such as Ix Tab ("she of the noose"), guider of the souls of sacrificial victims, of women who died in childbirth and of warriors.

In Aztec sacred belief, the supreme being was Ometeotl ("deity of dualities"), who was conceived of as having dual gender: part male, as Ometecuhtli, and part female, as Omecihuatl. Once Ometeotl had created the cosmos, the deity retired to Omeyocan ("place of duality"), but his/her spiritual power remained omnipresent, "his" masculinity being manifested in the forms of his male, solar divine offspring, and "her" femininity in her daughters, the earth goddesses. This dualistic creator deity could also be personified as Tonactecuhtli (male) and Tonacacihuatl (female). In many ways, this Mesoamerican concept corresponds to that of the Chinese *yin* and *yang*, representing similar views that despite the various functions traditionally accorded to male or female deities, the presence and interaction of both genders is vital to the creation and preservation of cosmic order. Another cosmogony is more directly related to the Goddess. It tells of the seizure of Tlaltecuhtli by Quetzalcoatl and Tezcatlipocca and the dismemberment of her body to form the earth and sky: "All the gods descended to console her and they ordained that from her would spring all the life necessary for the life of humans." It was said that she cried out at night for human blood (which she was given). Tlatecuhtli is represented as a monster or toad in a hocker (birth-giving) position, with teeth of flint blades. Her image was often carved on the bottom of sacred sculptures so that it would be in contact with the earth and thus enlist her cooperation. Clearly, Tlatecuhtli is the most terrible of primal earth goddesses, who provides sustenance to humans through her own sacrifice, but who demands comparable appeasement.

The primary Aztec mother goddess was acknowledged as Teteoinnan ("mother of sacred ones"). Although she received little direct worship, just as everything was regarded as being a part of Ometeotl, so all the lesser Aztec goddesses were believed to be manifestations of the various aspects of Teteoinnan. The Aztec goddess most closely linked to Teteoinnan was Toci ("our grandmother," also termed Tlallilyllo, "heart of the earth"), an earth deity who was worshipped during the Ochpaniztli

harvest festival. Like most Aztec goddesses, her benevolence was considered vital for the successful cultivation of maize, but with her Mayan sisters, she was also venerated as the patron of midwives and healers. When her worshippers wished to communicate with her, they frequently visited the sweatbath (*temascal*) to purify themselves. Toci herself is depicted with a black-lined face and wearing spools of cotton in her hair, attributes that link her to Tlazolteotl ("eater of filth," or Ixcuina, "cotton woman"), who was similarly represented. The fact that such goddesses wore ritual headdresses of cotton reflects the great value of this material to the Aztecs (for it would not grow in the Valley of Mexico) and thus the goddesses' elevated status, as well as their patronage of weaving. Like Toci, Tlazolteotl was regarded as a goddess of purification and was also symbolized by the sweatbath (from which people would emerge spiritually absolved and "reborn"), as well as by the grass broom with which she swept away transgressions. Again, however, she combined other conflicting functions, including those

Background: A pre-Columbian feline image from the Andes region.

Left: Aztec sacrificial rituals were performed to provide the gods with the human blood that they were believed to require for their sustenance. After their sacrifice, victims were rolled down the steps of the temple in a re-enactment of Huitzilopochtli's vengeful killing of his sister Coyolxauhqui, whom the circular stone at the base of the steps symbolized.

Above: Peasant Mother
(1929), by Mexican artist
David Alfaro Siqueiros,
is clearly influenced by
Christian images of the
Virgin and Child, yet it
retains the monumental
quality associated with the
powerful Mesoamerican
earth goddesses.

of sexuality and the powers of the moon (as one of the four or five lunar Ixcuiname goddesses), death and sorcery.

Both Toci and Tlazoteotl were earth goddesses of ancient origins, who might help their worshippers if it pleased them, but could also be quick to wreak punishment on those who offended them. In contrast, Xochiquetzal ("flower feather"/"flower quetzal bird") was the young and beautiful deity of love, beauty, flowers and sensuality, who also presided over the female spheres of weaving and childbirth. Her votive offerings, in the form of figurines, were ornamented with feathers, which, like Xochiquetzal, they wore in their hair. During the festival devoted to her (Hueypachtli), a priest would don the skin

of a sacrificed girl and sit at a loom to impersonate the goddess. Indeed, human sacrifice was central to most Aztec sacred rituals, for the gods were thought to require vast amounts of human blood for their nourishment. Aztec mythologies were characterized by horrifying violence, as seen in the story of Coatlicue ("the serpent skirt"). While she was sweeping clean Coatepec (the Aztec serpent/cosmic mountain), it was said that Coatlicue was impregnated with a dustball, which outraged her daughter Coyolxauhqui ("golden bells") and her 400 brothers, the Centzon Huitznahua, who fell upon their mother brandishing weapons. Coatlicue was struck a mortal blow, but before she died she gave birth to Huitzilopochtli (the Aztec supreme god). The symbolic representations of Coatlicue reveal the terrible powers that she embodied, yet also the pity that her brutal demise aroused: thus she was depicted wearing her serpent skirt (a fertility symbol), displaying sharpened claws, and with her body covered with human skulls, hearts and hands—all attributes of sacrifice—yet in her death agony she is shown without head and hands, with snakes (symbolizing blood) writhing from her neck and wrists.

Huitzilopochtli raised his mother to heaven, where she became the patron of flowers, and avenged her death by driving away his brothers and dismembering his sister, Coyolxauhqui, whose body he threw down the slopes of Coatepec (the mountain was recreated at Templo Mayor in the Aztec capital, Tenochtitlan). Coyolxauhqui's death was a symbolic blueprint for the Aztecs' sacrificial rituals, for, like her, their victims were often dismembered, or had their hearts torn out before their bodies were rolled to the bottom of the temple steps to land on the circular stone that represented the goddess. In symbolic terms, Coatlicue may represent the earth; Huitzilopochtli, the sun; Coyolxauhqui,

the moon; and the Centzon Huitzhahua, the stars. Coyolxauhqui's other symbols include the coyolli bells from which she derived her name and which were symbolically traced on her cheeks; indeed, some versions of the story say that after Huitzilopochtli learned that his sister had tried to protect their mother, he remorsefully placed her in the sky as the moon, where she lit up the night sky with her bells.

Several other Aztec goddesses were associated with the sky. Citlalicue ("star skirt"), for example, was the goddess of the Milky Way, who gave birth to a flintstone (the symbolic stone of fire and sacrifice) from which she created the gods, humans, the sun and the moon. Ilmatecuhtli ("woman of the old skirt," who was sometimes called Cihuacoatl, "woman snake"), was also equated with the Milky Way. She was represented as an old, white-garbed woman whose skirt was edged with white shells representing the stars (but also the womb); tobacco was especially sacred to her, as she was said to have created it. Other goddesses were venerated specifically as deities of vegetation. Mayahuel, for example, the personification of the maguey plant that produced the alcoholic beverage pulque, was envisaged as a multibreasted young woman whose milk was pulque, depicted within the plant bearing two ritual goblets. Despite her personification as a snake, Chicomecoatl ("seven serpent") ensured the growth of maize and was therefore shown carrying ears of corn, or wearing a corncob headdress. Chicomecoatl was the sister of the rain god Tlaloc—one of the most widely venerated Aztec deities— and his consort, Chalchihuitlicue ("jade skirt"), was another water deity; she had jurisdiction over fresh water and lakes, and thus also over childbirth. Her primary symbol was her skirt of jade, a stone especially venerated in Mesoamerica because its color was believed to symbolize the water, sky and vegetation. Another significant min-

eral was the black obsidian (of which Tezcatlipocca's magical smoking mirror was made), for it was believed to be the stone of sorcery and death. Thus the terrible skeletal death goddess Izpapalotl ("obsidian butterfly") was associated with this stone and depicted with wings tipped with either obsidian or flint; the butterfly or bat form that she assumed was also significant, for both creatures represented the souls of dead warriors in Aztec belief.

On a superficial level, it may seem that the Mayan and Aztec goddesses display conflicting characteristics, yet this is not really the case: despite the apparently striking contrast between the relatively gentle, lunar, Mayan female deities and the bloodthirsty, violent, earth Aztec goddesses, each tradition mirrors the ancient and universal attributes associated with the Goddess, but with the aspect most relevant to her worshippers given greater emphasis. Indeed, it is in their symbols that their fundamental similarity is manifested.

Background: The butterfly, an emblem of the Aztec goddess of death.

Below: The Mexican painter José Clemente Orozco's dynamic work Maternity (1923) emphasizes the Christian, Madonna-like symbolism of the mother and child at the center of this image by surrounding the pair with an angelic sorority, manifesting solidarity with the maternal principle.

The Goddess Reinterpreted

As we have seen, in ancient times the Goddess was a central mythological figure in most of the world's many sacred beliefs and, where these beliefs have endured, she remains the subject of intense devotion. It is in the Western mindset alone, which has so long been conditioned by the patriarchal beliefs of the Judeo-Christian tradition, that the Goddess *per se* is considered an alien concept, her worship often regarded patronizingly as part of those "primitive" or exotic faiths that have yet to experience the enlightenment offered solely by the Judeo-Christian God. Islam, too, which shares many elements of the Judeo-Christian tradition, acknowledges the masculine Allah as its only deity. When one considers that, in terms of the number of its followers, Christianity (with two billion adherents) is the most widespread world religion, followed closely by Islam (with just over a billion adherents), it appears that the Goddess has been effectively excluded from the spiritual life of most of the world's people. Yet this is not altogether the case, for the Goddess has survived (albeit in disguise) even within these rigidly monotheistic faiths, while during the twentieth century the various components of the New Age movement have turned their backs on the traditional teachings of Western religion in their search for spiritual fulfillment, thereby reviving her worship. Thus the Goddess is now re-emerging into the consciousness of the West two millennia after her banishment, demonstrating that the unconscious mind feels itself incomplete without her archetypal presence.

THE JUDEO-CHRISTIAN TRADITION

The fact that there is no place for the Goddess in the Judeo-Christian tradition is spelled out clearly in the Old Testament. The primeval vacuum from which the components of the universe were created, the fashioning of the first human from clay—all these actions that were traditionally the province of the Goddess are detailed, yet the creator deity of Genesis is unambiguously identified as a male god. The story of the Fall of humankind also features such crucial symbols of the Goddess as the apple-bearing tree of knowledge (or life) that grows in the garden of paradise, as well as the serpent. Yet, consistent with the authorship that condemns the worship of the goddess Ashtoreth, in the Old Testament these symbols are denied their ancient and positive

Opposite: Lochner's delightful treatment of the Madonna and Child in The Virgin of the Rose Garden *(1448) accords the "Mystical Rose" a predominant position within the canvas, surrounded by cherubic angels, while God and the Holy Spirit (symbolized by the dove) look down on her in benediction.*

Left: Botticelli's Return of Judith *(1472). Within the Apocrypha of the Old Testament, Judith is celebrated as a heroine (the highest status accorded women in the Pentateuch) who ended the Babylonian siege of the Jewish people by lulling the general Holofernes into a false sense of security and then decapitating him.*

This page: Such Christian artists as Raphael (above, left) and Cranach (above, right), portrayed Eve as the cause of humankind's Fall. Thus the serpent, apple and tree, ancient fertility symbols, were debased. Said to have been formed from the rib of Adam (as illustrated by Raphael, right), Eve was denied the creative function ascribed to ancient goddesses.

life-affirming significance. They are instead, demonized: the apples of knowledge are a source of culpability, the snake is the trickster who precipitates the fall from grace, and Eve is the weak and credulous woman whose disobedience to God brings the inherited stigma of original sin upon humanity. As a result, not only is the Goddess extirpated from the Judeo-Christian credo, her serpent symbol equated with the devil, but woman is cursed (with menstruation and the agony of childbirth), and relegated to a position subordinate to that of man.

This is the orthodox view of the Goddess and her attributes in Judaism, Christianity, and also Islam, which accepts many aspects of the Old Testament. Yet even within these strictly monotheistic faiths, we may still catch glimpses of the Goddess that were never entirely eradicated among their more unorthodox adherents. Thus, for example, Kabbalistic Jews believed that Hokmah (symbolized as a *sephiroth* on the Kabbalistic tree of life) was God's feminine principle, whom Gnostic Christians equated with Sophia ("wisdom") and whose symbol was the dove that later personified the Holy Spirit. Of the ten *sephira* on the Kabbalistic tree of life, who were believed to collectively represent God's divine characteristics, some were especially identified with aspects of the Goddess: Binah ("understanding," symbolized by the color black), Tiphereth ("magnificence," associated with the sun, moon and planet Venus) and Malkuth ("queen," represented by the throne of justice). Kabbalism and Gnosticism respected the female principle as a vital part of divinity; Islamic traditions perhaps less so, but it should be noted that the Prophet's daughter, Fatima, was said by some to have given birth to her sons from her thigh—a legend that may equate her with the virgin Goddess, and that has parallels with the nativities of both Buddha and Christ.

Indeed, among all of these related monotheistic traditions, it is the Virgin Mary who, by virtue of the veneration she inspires, as well as the nature of her symbolic attributes, assumes enormous significance in any discussion of the history of the worship and symbols of the Goddess. The fact that "Our Lady" (a title she shares with many ancient goddesses) is not a goddess in Christian dogma cannot be overemphasized. However, despite this *caveat*, in terms of aspects of her veneration and in her artistic representations she has come to assume many of the archetypal characteristics and attributes of the benevolent mother goddess. It may also be significant that the Church discouraged her cult for centuries, fearing that it detracted from the adoration of God, but was eventually forced to give way in the face of her profound and ineradicable popularity among Christians.

Left: The Kabbalistic Tree of Life contains ten sephira, *each of which is said to be an aspect of the godhead. This Jewish mystical tradition, along with Christian Gnosticism, preserved the importance of the masculine/feminine dualism that was banished by the Jewish and Christian orthodoxies.*

Left: This languid Turkish depiction of Eve apparently confirms the traditional Islamic (as well as the Christian and Jewish) view of the first woman and her female descendants as dangerous seductresses and temptresses, a result of the conscious denigration of the feminine principle as embodied by the Goddess.

Annunciation; the veil of modesty that affirms her chastity; and the crescent moon—the symbol of so many virgin goddesses, including Artemis/Diana. As the mother of Christ (or *theotokos*— "god-bearer," as she has been known since the fifth century), she is shown as the Madonna who nurses the Christ Child (in a striking parallel with the more ancient representations of Isis and Horus). As the Lady of Mercy (*Misericord*), her blue cloak shelters the faithful, its color that of the water over which ancient goddesses ruled. In fact, her name is derived from the Latin *mare*: sea. She may also be symbolized by the star, for like Isis, Aphrodite/Venus, and many Mesopotamian goddesses, she is the star of the sea (*Stella Maris*). She shares Aphrodite's rose attribute, too: Christians call her the Mystical Rose, sprung from the root of

Above: *In* Immaculate Virgin *(1880), Bustoz, depicted Mary surrounded by twelve stars.* **Right:** *Del Sarto's* Assumption of the Virgin *(1526) illustrates Mary's bodily ascension into heaven.* **Background:** *An emblem of Mary as the "Mystical Rose."*

In the Christian tradition, Mary was not only the virgin mother of Christ, but was conceived of human parents free of original sin. This doctrine of the Immaculate Conception identifies her as the only person besides Christ whose nature was untainted by sinful tendencies. Thus her attributes include the lily (in Christianity a symbol of purity, but in other traditions, one of fertility), which the archangel Gabriel often bears in images of the

Jesse, Christ's ancestor and namesake. As such, her most important symbol is the rosary, the string of devotional beads used as an aid to prayer, whose "decades" (series of ten beads) recall significant events of Mary's life and afterlife.

Parallels may be drawn between the Virgin Mary and the Goddess and between other female saints (particularly in the Celtic Christian tradition) and specific aspects of the Goddess. Indeed, the peculiar fusion of Celtic sacred belief and Christianity may also be seen in medieval tales of the Holy Grail, the cup which Christ was said to have used during the Last Supper, and in which Joseph of Arimathea caught the blood flowing from His wounds as He hung upon the cross. Eternally sought, the Grail is believed to have miraculous powers of healing and redemption, as the cauldron

of the Celtic Goddess promised the gift of life and renewal. Thus the Goddess and her symbols are very much present in Christian tradition; and it is perhaps also significant that the body of Christian adherents is termed "Mother Church." And in sacred art, the almond-shaped oval mandorlas enclosing many figures have affinity with traditional symbols of female genitalia, like the *yoni* that represents the Hindu Goddess.

Above: The Virgin and Child in Raphael's Sistine Madonna *(1512). Mary wears her traditional blue mantle.* **Left:** *In Botticelli's* The Annunciation *(1481), Mary's role as "god-bearer" links her with the Goddess who bestows life.*

MODERN GODDESS CULTS

Since Christianity absorbed many of the legends and attributes associated with the Goddess, she remained accessible to some degree, but not enough to satisfy many people of the Western tradition. During the twentieth century, they have instigated a remarkable and relatively widespread re-evaluation of the tenets of several established faiths. This was prompted partly by the rise of the feminist movement, which rejects the subordinate role traditionally ascribed to women, and partly by the growth of the Green environmental movement, which holds that the Earth and its resources are to be respected and not exploited. Under the umbrella name of the New Age movement, such views are becoming increasingly accepted: all advocate a return to the ancient wisdom and spirituality of pagan times, and all celebrate the power of femininity and the sanctity of nature, thereby according the principles traditionally embodied by the Goddess a pre-eminent position.

Opposite: *The Virgin and Child as objects of veneration in the Christian East; the tree of life, or fertility, or a genealogical "family tree"; Daphne, who was saved from defilement by Gaia, and turned into a laurel tree.*
Above: *Primavera (1478) by Botticelli represents the burgeoning of nature and the powers of fertility inherent in the Goddess.*
Left: *Hecate, as depicted by William Blake, surrounded by her creatures of the night, including a bat, owl and night-mare.*

Right: *This twentieth-century woman lounges seductively on a crescent moon—the symbol of countless goddesses, as well as of Christianity's Virgin Mary. Despite the Goddess's debasement in the Western world, her image and attributes retain their powerful archetypal significance.*
Right: *New York's most famous Statue of Liberty: this goddesslike guardian of democracy evokes the values of individual and collective freedom, and has become an American icon.*

Certain modern reconstructions of ancient faiths give such concepts special importance, and two movements are primarily responsible for the resurgence of Goddess worship: neopaganism and Wiccanism (or the Dianic movement). Although neopagans believe that the principles of masculinity (personified as the Horned God) and femininity (represented by the Goddess) are both universally present and, indeed, essential, the Goddess is often emphasized because of her undisputed dominance of the natural world, as a mother, as nature, and as presider over death and rebirth. Acknowledging as they do the sanctity of nature and the many divine forces at work in the world, the neopagans have turned back to ancient sacred

beliefs in pantheism, polytheism and animism. These tenets go hand in hand with those of eco-feminism, or of planetary consciousness, which may be summed up in biologist James E. Lovelock's Gaia Hypothesis, first postulated in the 1970s. Essentially, Lovelock proposed the theory, based on exhaustive scientific research, that the Earth is a self-regulating entity, which appears to adjust its biological components so as to maintain a remarkably consistent level of homeostasis, allowing life forms to exist despite the presence of potentially destructive external factors. It is appropriate that the name Gaia Hypothesis, which was proposed by novelist William Golding, links the Earth's hypothetical consciousness with the mother goddess of the Greeks, whose body was believed to form it.

In many respects, the beliefs and rituals of neopaganism are closely linked with those of both the Dianic tradition and Wiccanism, whose adherents—modern-day witches—can at last practice their ancient rites after centuries of the most terrible persecution. For, just as the Goddess was increasingly denigrated by Christianity, so from medieval times her

symbolic attributes of fertility took on sinister connotations. Her serpent became the form of the Devil (and in the twentieth century, thanks to the influence of Sigmund Freud, a phallic symbol), while cats, toads and dogs were regarded as demonic familiars. Herbology was considered less a natural form of healing than the preparation of Satanic potions. Thus the Goddess as crone became a witch, her cauldron of abundance used for destructive purposes and her manifold incarnations condemned as evidence of the shape-shifting powers of evil. Today, however, Wiccanists practice their rituals as a celebration of the powers of the Goddess, communing with her in the open air (just as the Celts worshipped her in sacred groves) within magic circles (the symbol of integration and the womb) and channeling her wisdom in trancelike states (a skill that has never been abandoned in such sacred traditions as shamanism). Such spiritual movements venerate a multitude of Goddess aspects, but the ancient trinity of virgin, mother and crone (in the Dianic tradition called Diana, Selene and Hecate, all aspects of the moon) are the three most profound archetypes.

While neopaganism and Wiccanism are the leading exponents of modern Goddess worship, it seems that she is re-emerging into humanity's conscious even when she is not directly worshipped. One example is that of the "croning ceremonies" presided over by the Crones Council of North America (which is not associated with any spiritual movement). They have sought, since 1982, to restore to older women their ancient status of "wise women." During such ceremonies, women are celebrated as "crones" in the presence of a corresponding effigy of the Goddess. Their foreheads are daubed with ash, and they receive rainbow-hued stoles and amethysts as symbols of both the crone Goddess and their initiation. In Hong

Left: The water nymphs of Greco-Roman mythology are evoked by this twentieth-century figure, who unconsciously echoes the Goddess's age-old power over fertility and water. **Below:** *Neopagans reaffirm the beliefs of ancient religions such as Druidism—illustrated by this romanticized image of a mistletoe-crowned maiden bearing a sickle—and have played a part in restoring the Goddess to her former eminence.*

Right: Even in those cultures in which the Goddess is no longer worshipped, female figures may assume symbolic and inspirational importance, as illustrated by Delacroix's Liberty Leading the People *(1830), an allegory of the French Revolution.* **Below, right:** *Renoir's* Diana *(1867) represents the Roman goddess with her traditional symbols, including creatures of the hunt and the crescent-shaped bow.* **Opposite:** *Surrealist artists, in such works as Magritte's* Black Magic *(1835), top left, and Vines's* Mujer [Woman] *(1929), below, celebrate the beauty of the female body, whose life-giving powers, top right, inspired our ancient ancestors to worship the Goddess rather than a god.*

Kong, in 1997, demonstrators commemorated the crushing of the fledgling democratic movement in Beijing's Tiananmen Square (1989) by marching on China's unofficial embassy—the offices of the news agency Xinhua—to place a gigantic portrait of the Goddess of Democracy over the gates. This emblem of the 1989 protest movement was similar in form to the Statue of Liberty, the American symbol of democratic freedom. One might venture to say that in this choice of symbol, the protesters were suggesting that benevolent qualities represented by the Goddess were sorely missing in the patriarchal Chinese political arena.

Indeed, many ancient truths are only now being recognized in the Western world, although they have never been forgotten in many, perhaps wiser, sacred traditions—notably, the fact that both masculine and feminine principles are

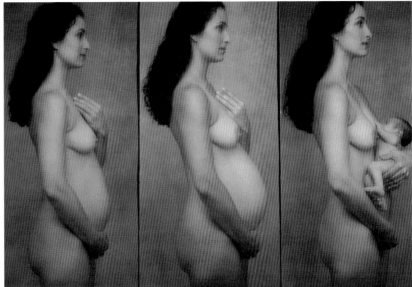

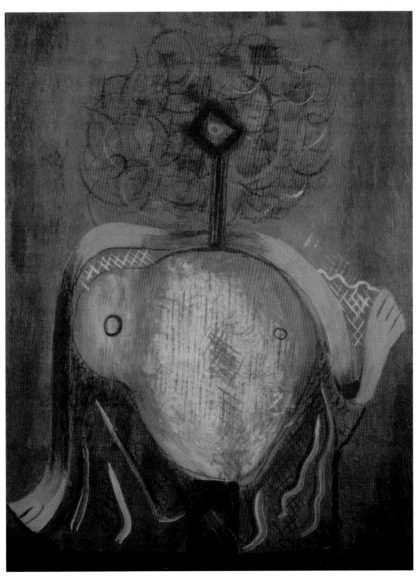

needed in order to achieve holistic harmony. Neither one is superior to the other,
nor are they in opposition: rather, they
complement each other and, when united,
achieve perfection. Too long has the feminine, symbolized by the Goddess herself,
been suppressed by the masculine—the
God—but she is finally re-emerging into
the Western psyche. And for many
observers, it is not before time. As Laurens
van der Post commented in his 1990
introduction to Anne Baring and Jules
Cashford's enlightening study *The Myth
of the Goddess*: "The horizon behind us is
littered with the rubble of civilizations
which have failed to renew themselves,
have failed a challenge somehow to transcend their opposites in something that
will combine in balance both the masculine and feminine and, in their union, create something greater than the sum of
their parts."

BIBLIOGRAPHY

Bonnie S. Anderson and Judith P. Zinsser, *A History of Their Own: Women in Europe from Prehistory to the Present*, vol. I, Penguin Books, Harmondsworth, 1990.

Martha Ann and Dorothy Myers Imel, *Goddesses in World Mythology: A Biographical Dictionary*, Oxford University Press, Oxford, 1993.

Norman Bancroft-Hunt, *Native Americans: The Life and Culture of the North American Indian*, Chartwell Books, Edison, N.J., 1996.

Anne Baring and Jules Cashford, *The Myth of the Goddess: Evolution of an Image*, Penguin Arkana Ltd., Harmondsworth, 1993.

Udo Becker (ed.), *The Element Encyclopedia of Symbols*, Element Books Ltd., Shaftesbury, 1994.

Robert E. Bell, *Women of Classical Mythology: A Biographical Dictionary*, Oxford University Press, Oxford, 1991.

Janet and Colin Bord, *Dictionary of Earth Mysteries*, Thorsons, HarperCollins Publishers, London, 1996.

John Bowker, *World Religions: The Great Faiths Explored and Explained*, Dorling Kindersley, London, 1997.

Brian Branston, *The Lost Gods of England*, Constable and Company Ltd, London, 1993.

Cottie Burland, *North American Indian Mythology*, Chancellor Press, London, 1996.

Joseph Campbell, *The Mythic Image*, Princeton Univesity Press, Princeton, N.J., 1974.

Wally Caruana, *Aboriginal Art*, Thames & Hudson Ltd., London, 1993.

Richard Cavendish (ed.), *Mythology: An Illustrated Encyclopedia*, Macdonald & Co. (Publishers) Ltd., London, 1991.

Jean Chevalier and Alain Gheerbrant, *The Penguin Dictionary of Symbols*, Penguin Books Ltd., Harmondsworth, 1996.

J. E. Cirlot, *A Dictionary of Symbols*, Routledge, London, 1995.

Roger Cook, *The Tree of Life: Image for the Cosmos*, Thames & Hudson Ltd., London, 1974.

J. C. Cooper, *An Illustrated Encyclopaedia of Traditional Symbols*, Thames & Hudson Ltd., London, 1978.

J. C. Cooper (ed.), *Brewer's Book of Myth and Legend*, Helicon Publishing Ltd., Oxford, 1995.

G. Duchet-Suchaux and M. Pastoureau, *The Bible and the Saints*, Flammarion, Paris, 1994.

David Fontana, *The Secret Language of Symbols: A Visual Key to Symbols and Their Meanings*, Pavilion Books Ltd., London, 1993.

Sir James Frazer, *The Golden Bough*, Wordsworth Editions Ltd., London, 1993.

Clare Gibson, *Signs and Symbols*, Saraband Inc., Rowayton, Conn., 1996.

Marija Gimbutas, *The Goddesses and Gods of Old Europe: Myths and Cult Images*, Thames & Hudson Ltd., London, 1996.

————, *The Language of the Goddess*, Thames & Hudson Ltd., London, 1992.

Rosemary Goring (ed.), *The Wordsworth Dictionary of Beliefs and Religions*, Wordsworth Editions Ltd., Ware, 1995.

Miranda J. Green, *Dictionary of Celtic Myth and Legend*, Thames & Hudson Ltd., London, 1992.

Rosemary Ellen Guiley, *Encyclopedia of Mystical and Paranormal Experience*, HarperCollins Publishers, New York, 1991.

James Hall, *Hall's Illustrated Dictionary of Symbols in Eastern and Western Art*, John Murray (Publishers) Ltd., London, 1994.

John R. Hinells (ed.), *The Penguin Dictionary of Religions*, Penguin Books Ltd., Harmondsworth, 1984.

Jessica Hodge, *Who's Who in Classical Mythology*, Bison Books Ltd., London, 1995.

Nadia Julien, *The Mammoth Dictionary of Symbols: Understanding the Hidden Language of Symbols*, Robinson Publishing, London, 1996.

Jan Knappert, *Pacific Mythology: An Encyclopedia of Myth and Legend*, Diamond Books, London, 1995.

John Laing and David Wire, *The Encyclopedia of Signs and Symbols*, Studio Editions Ltd., London, 1993.

Bernard Lewis (ed.), *The World of Islam: Faith, People, Culture*, Thames & Hudson Ltd., London, 1994.

Carl G. Liungman, *Dictionary of Symbols*, W. W. Norton & Co., New York, 1994.

Caitlin Matthews, *The Elements of the Celtic Tradition*, Element Books Ltd., Shaftesbury, 1989.

Rosalind Miles, *The Women's History of the World*, HarperCollins Publishers, London, 1993.

Mary Miller and Karl Taube, *The Gods and Symbols of Ancient Mexico and the Maya: An Illustrated Dictionary of Mesoamerican Religion*, Thames & Hudson Ltd., London, 1993.

Alexander S. Murray, *Who's Who in Mythology: Classic Guide to the Ancient World*, Bracken Books, London, 1994.

Geoffrey Parrinder, *African Mythology*, Chancellor Press, London, 1996.

T. W. Rolleston, *Celtic Myths and Legends*, Studio Editions, London (undated).

Alistair Shearer, *Buddha: The Intelligent Heart*, Thames & Hudson Ltd., London, 1992.

Alan Unterman, *Dictionary of Jewish Lore and Legend*, Thames & Hudson Ltd., London, 1991.

Barbara G. Walker, *The Woman's Dictionary of Symbols and Sacred Objects*, Pandora, London, 1995.

Derek Walters, *Chinese Mythology: An Encyclopedia of Myth and Legend*, Diamond Books, London, 1995.

INDEX

*Page numbers in **boldface** type refer to illustrations.*

111

ACKNOWLEDGEMENTS

This book is dedicated to Marianne Gibson. The publisher would like to thank the following individuals for their assistance in the preparation of this book: Sara Hunt and Robin Sommer, editors; Nicola Gillies, assistant editor and photo research; Charles J. Ziga, art director; Wendy Ciaccia, graphic designer; Keith Hunt, illustrator; and Lisa Langone Desautels, indexer. Grateful acknowledgement is also made to the following individuals and institutions for permission to reproduce pictures in this book: **AKG, London:** 6, 8l, 9t, 19, 29t, 33b, 34l, 35l, 66, 67r, 92b, 96, 106t; **Corbis-Bettmann:** 103b, 105b; **CorelDraw:** 7, 12, 24, 27, 28, 29b, 31, 32, 33t, 36, 37r, 38b, 49b, 53br, 62, 64, 65, 68t, 69t, 82, 102t; **Digital Vision:** 16b, 77t; **FPG International:** 15b (© James Porto 1992), 49t (© H. Richard Johnston 1993), 53t (© Gary Buss 1994), 83 (©Yamada Toyohiro 1992), 107tr (© Joyce Tenneson 1993); **Historic Scotland, Ancient Monuments Division:** 50t; **Library of Congress, Prints and Photographs Division:** 87b, 88, 93; **Mary Evans Picture Library:** 42, 44b, 47, 48t; **Metropolitan Museum of Art, Fletcher Fund, 1935:** 17; **Planet Art:** 8r, 9b, 10, 11, 14, 20, 30, 37l, 39, 40, 41, 50b, 51t, 54, 55, 59, 60, 61, 63, 69b, 70, 71b, 73, 74, 75, 75b, 77b, 81, 85, 89, 90, 94, 95, 97, 98, 99, 100, 101, 102br & bl, 103t, 104t, 105t, 106b, 107tl &b; © **Jeanne Walker Rorex:** 13; **Saraband Image Library:** 21, 26, 48, 56, 68b, 71t; © **Michael Tincher:** 15t, 86b, 87t; **Yerke's Observatory, University of Chicago:** 25; © **Charles J. Ziga:** 15t, 18, 22, 38t, 58t, 72, 78b, 79, 80, 84, 86t, 91, 92t, 104.